T0354399

Using
EXCEL
IN THE
Classroom

**CORWIN
PRESS**

The Corwin Press logo—a raven striding across an open book—represents the happy union of courage and learning. We are a professional-level publisher of books and journals for K–12 educators, and we are committed to creating and providing resources that embody these qualities. Corwin's motto is "Success for All Learners."

Using EXCEL IN THE Classroom

Jennifer Summerville

Jean Morrow

Dusti Howell

With contributions from:

Renee M. Eggers

Deanne Howell

CORWIN PRESS, INC.
A Sage Publications Company
Thousand Oaks, California

Copyright © 2002 by Corwin Press, Inc.

All rights reserved. When forms and sample documents are included, their use is authorized only by educators, local school sites, and/or noncommercial entities who have purchased the book. Except for that usage, no part of this book may be reproduced or utilized in any form or by any means, electronic or mechanical, including photocopying, recording, or by any information storage and retrieval system, without permission in writing from the publisher.

For information:

Corwin Press, Inc.
A Sage Publications Company
2455 Teller Road
Thousand Oaks, California 91320
E-mail: order@corwinpress.com

Sage Publications Ltd.
6 Bonhill Street
London EC2A 4PU
United Kingdom

Sage Publications India Pvt. Ltd.
M-32 Market
Greater Kailash I
New Delhi 110 048 India

Printed in the United States of America

Library of Congress Cataloging-in-Publication Data

Using Excel in the classroom / by Jennifer Summerville ... [et al.].
    p. cm.
  Includes index.
  ISBN 0-7619-7879-8 (c) — ISBN 0-7619-7880-1 (p)
  1. Microsoft Excel (Computer file) 2. Computer managed instruction. 3. Computer-assisted instruction. I. Summerville, Jennifer.
 LB1028.46 .U82 2002
 005.369—dc21

                    2001005564

This book is printed on acid-free paper.

02   03   04   05   06   07   7   6   5   4   3   2   1

Acquisitions Editor:	Robb Clouse
Associate Editor:	Kylee Liegl
Editorial Assistant:	Erin Buchanan
Production Editor:	Olivia Weber
Typesetter/Designer:	Larry K. Bramble
Copy Editor:	Denise McIntyre
Cover Designer:	Tracy E. Miller

Contents

Preface

Welcome to *Using Excel in the Classroom*. If you want to create more dynamic classroom lessons by integrating the use of spreadsheets in your teaching and have some fun learning, this book is for you. This book is designed to give you immediate results using either Windows or Macintosh platforms. You will also learn the fundamentals of creating powerful spreadsheets that enhance learning in your classroom.

Acknowledgments

We would like to extend our sincere appreciation to our colleagues in the field and in the classroom who read this text, tested our ideas, and provided feedback and support during the editorial process.

The following reviewers are gratefully acknowledged:

Gregg Elder
Teacher-Librarian,
   Technical Chair
Evergreen Middle School
Everett, WA

Robin Van Heyningen
Teacher
White River High School
Buckley, WA

Kristen L. Blake
Teacher
La Habra High School
La Habra, CA

Joe Meersman
Teacher
Toppenish High School
Toppenish, WA

Richard J. Marchesani
Assistant Professor of Education
Elmira College
Elmira, NY

Eric Alm
Teacher
Jenkins High School
Chewelah, WA

Katherine Avila
Teacher
Tewksbury Memorial High School
Tewksbury, MA

Ken Martin
Coordinator of Curriculum and Instruction
University of Cincinnati
College of Education
Cincinnati, OH

Blake West
District Coordinating Teacher for
   Technology
Blue Valley Schools
Overland Park, KS

Ellen Thompson
Teacher
Horizon Elementary School
Madison, AL

Fred MacDonald
Program Officer
Standards of Practice and Education
Ontario College of Teachers
Toronto, Ontario, Canada

Tawn Rundle
Teacher/Elementary Technology
   Coordinator
Laverne Public Schools
Laverne, OR

Note: All screen shots are reprinted
by permission of Microsoft Corporation.

The Microsoft Excel program is a registered trademark of Microsoft Corporation in the United States and/or other countries. All brand names and product names used in this book are trade names, service marks, trademarks, or registered trademarks of their respective owners. The authors are not associated with Microsoft or any other product or vendor mentioned in this book.

All terms mentioned in this book that are known to be trademarks have been appropriately capitalized. Rather than list all the names and entities that own the trademarks or insert a trademark symbol with each mention of the trademarked name, the authors and publisher state that they are using the names only for editorial purposes and to the benefit of the trademark owner with no intention of infringing upon that mark.

The authors have attempted to include trademark information for screen shots, icons, clip art, and Office Assistants referred to in this book. Although the authors have made reasonable efforts in gathering this information, they cannot guarantee its accuracy.

About the Authors

Jennifer Summerville is Assistant Professor of Instructional Design and Technology at Emporia State University. She received a master's in computer education and cognitive systems from the University of North Texas and a PhD in educational technology with emphases in distance education, instructional design, and interactive multimedia design from the University of Northern Colorado. She specializes in instructional design, distance education, and instructional media design. Her research interests include integration of technology in the K-12 classroom, learner-centered issues in distance education, and cognitive and personality issues in the design and development of instruction.

Jean Morrow, OSM, EdD, has 40 years of classroom teaching experience at all levels, from first grade through university. She has been a member of Servants of Mary since 1958. She earned a master's degree in mathematics education from the University of Detroit and a doctorate in instructional design and technology from Boston University. The coauthor of two books on mathematics instruction, she is a frequent speaker at state and national meetings. Her favorite theme for those talks is the integration of technology and problem solving. Most recently, Jean has been teaching classes over the Internet for Emporia State University in Emporia, Kansas. Jean serves on the Board of Examiners for the National Council for the Accreditation of Teacher Education. In 1998, she was given the Distinguished Clinician Award in Teacher Education by the Association of Teacher Educators.

Dusti D. Howell earned a PhD in curriculum and instruction with an emphasis in educational communications and technology and a PhD minor in educational psychology from the University of Wisconsin–Madison. He is currently teaching at Emporia State University in the Instructional Design and Technology Department. His expertise includes high-tech study skills and digital learning strategies, multimedia, and video production. He teaches online courses including "Powerful Presentations in PowerPoint" and "Fundamental 4Mat Training."

He has taught every grade level from first grade through graduate school. He is currently president of the local chapter of Phi Delta Kappa.

Renee M. Eggers is Assistant Professor at Youngstown State University, where she teaches undergraduate and graduate courses on educational technology. She is the author of several articles dealing with use and integration of technology in educational situations. In addition to being a member of the Technology Commission for the Association of Teacher Educators, she is a member of Ohio's Statewide Technology Framework Committee.

Deanne K. Howell teaches professional development courses for university faculty and staff. She conducts professional development workshops, online courses, and classes for Emporia State University. Deanne holds a master's degree in science education from the University of Wisconsin–Madison. She has taught in public, private, and international schools.

Understanding Microsoft® Excel

T his book covers Windows versions 2000 and 97 and Macintosh versions 2001 and 98. The good news is that for regular users of spreadsheets, there are only minor differences between any of these versions. Thus, if you learn on one, you will be able to easily transfer this knowledge to any of the other packages. Furthermore, many of the commands are identical or very similar in each of the other programs. There are, however, a few differences. For example, Microsoft Excel 2001 has a different toolbar and icons. One other important difference between the Macintosh and Windows version is the keyboard shortcuts: Windows uses the **Ctrl** key, the equivalent of the **Command ⌘** key on the Macintosh. While holding down **Ctrl** or **Command,** press down on a particular key (e.g., "S" for "Save") to execute a task. The directions for this shortcut look like this: **Ctrl/⌘+S.**

Most of the directions in this book work for all four versions. When there are differences, look for the following:

WIN or WINDOWS	Windows versions 97 and 2000 only
MAC or MACINTOSH	Macintosh versions 98 and 2001 only

WIN 97   Windows version 97 only

WIN 00   Windows 2000 only

MAC 98   Macintosh version 98 only

MAC 01   Macintosh version 2001 only

What Excel Version Am I Using?

WINDOWS

After opening Excel, select **Help** from the top of the menu and choose **About Microsoft Excel** from the drop-down menu. A dialog box that contains information about the particular version of Microsoft Excel on your computer will appear (Figure 1.1). To return to the normal screen, click on the **Close** button or select **OK**.

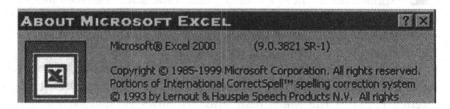

Figure 1.1   About Microsoft Excel

MACINTOSH

Macintosh users can obtain similar information by clicking on the **Apple Menu** (top left of screen) and selecting **About Microsoft Excel.**

Uses and Features

Excel has numerous uses in the classroom, for example:

- ▶ Create a gradebook.

- ▶ Develop budget reports.

- ▶ Design lessons for teaching a variety of mathematical concepts.

- ▶ Analyze the results of science experiments.

- ▶ Produce charts and graphs to illustrate data in spreadsheets.

In addition, although beyond the scope of this book, it is nearly as easy to create spreadsheets to put on a Web page as it is to make regular spreadsheet files. As you will find out, Excel is a very versatile tool for both teachers and students.

Starting Excel

WINDOWS

There are several ways to "start" or open Microsoft Excel. The most common way is to put your cursor on the **Start** button on the far left of the toolbar at the bottom of the screen. Hold down the left mouse button and the **Start** window will pop up. Continue holding the button down while scrolling up to the folder **Programs** to open the menu of programs on your computer. Double click on **Microsoft Excel** to open the application. (See Figure 1.2.)

An alternative way to start the program is to find the **Office Shortcut Bar,** which may be available on your desktop. In this case, simply click on the **Excel** icon, and the program will open.

Observe the three small controls in the upper right corner. Clicking on the middle icon, a "full window," makes the active window full screen. Clicking on the middle icon, shown as "overlapping windows," makes the window less than full screen and also means you can use the Microsoft Windows "drag" feature to create a window of any size. The left icon or "bar" will collapse the screen into the taskbar at the bottom of your desktop. The far right "X" will close the window, which also closes Microsoft Excel.

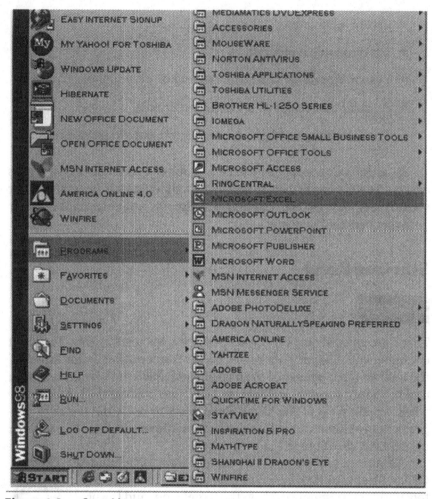

Figure 1.2 Start Menu

MACINTOSH

Double click the **Hard Drive**—often labeled **Macintosh HD**—icon at the top right of the screen to bring up the Macintosh Hard Drive window that indicates all of the programs and documents stored on your computer's hard drive.

1. Double click on the **Microsoft Office** folder. The Microsoft Office window will appear.

2. Double click on the icon labeled **Microsoft Excel.**

If you have used Microsoft Excel recently, click on the **Apple** menu located at the top left of the screen to bring down the menu. Go down to **Recent Applications** and click **Microsoft Excel** to open the application.

The top row of the work area window is called the **Title Bar.** The **Close Box** on the far left of this bar closes the window when clicked. Note: It does not close Excel—it is still open when the Application menu in the top right corner of the screen is selected. Two other buttons are located on the far right side of the title bar. The first is the **Zoom box** that changes the size of the window when clicked. The **Collapse box** in the far right corner collapses the window but leaves the title bar open on the screen.

Excel Toolbars

The screen will be gray, and selected features will not be shown until you have actually opened a workbook. The top of the screen shows the *Menu* bar, *Standard* and *Formatting* toolbars. Excel is highly customizable, and your screen may show different items at the top. To make Excel look like the screens in this book, put the cursor on **View** on the menu bar and scroll down to **Toolbars.**

Be sure to have only **Standard** and **Formatting** checked.

Although Excel offers several options to open a file, the "quick start" way is to select the **New Blank Document** icon. This opens a "clean" new page, which is called a workbook. Each "page" of the workbook is known as a worksheet. You can see the tabs for three sheets at the lower left of the Excel screen.

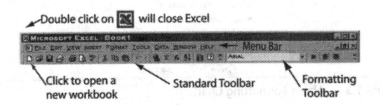

The most frequently used toolbar items are the **New Blank Document, Open, Save,** and **Print** icons. These functions are on the left side of the toolbar.

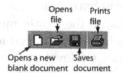

Experiment with the Windows "drag" feature. Put the cursor in any corner (**MAC:** only bottom right) of the window until it becomes an angled arrow. By touching the mouse button, you can "drag" the window to any size.

HELP!

Help may be only a mouse click away. Besides using this book, you'll be pleased to know that Excel has provided several major ways to get help. First, Excel includes the "Office Assistant," which can show up nearly anywhere on your window. Besides that, it will occasionally "wink" at you and make faces. The Windows Office Assistant is active by default (automatically). Click on the Office Assistant and a screen will appear asking, "What would you like to do?"

1. Type in "Chart" and press **Enter/Return** (or click on **Search**), and the bulleted items will focus on chart items.

2. Selecting *About Formatting Charts* from the list of topics brings up an answer window on the right side of the screen. (**MAC 01:** Click on the *See More . . .* option.)

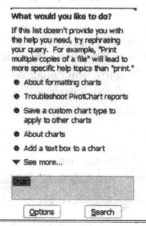

Figure 1.3   About Formatting Charts

The Mac Office Assistant looks like a "friendly computer," and by clicking on it you will be able to type in a question.

Excel has thousands of topics available, and many answers have several suggestions and links to "additional resources."

To open the Office Assistant when it is not visible, click on the **Microsoft Excel Help** icon on the *Standard* toolbar. Second, Microsoft Excel also lets you hide the Office Assistant. This option is available by *right* clicking (**MAC: Ctrl + Click**) on the Office Assistant, and selecting *Hide* or *Hide Assistant* from the drop-down menu.

When you select **Help > Microsoft Excel Help** you will see a different help screen. The following screen shows "formula" as a keyword on the *Index* tab.

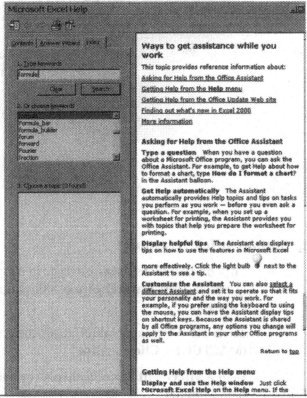

Figure 1.4   Microsoft Excel Help

Quick Review

▶ **What Excel Version Am I Using?**

WIN: Help > About Microsoft Excel

MAC: Apple > About Microsoft Excel

▶ **Launching Excel**

WIN: **Start > Programs > Excel**

MAC: Double click on **Hard drive** icon > double click on
             MS Office folder > double click on **Excel**

▶ **Standard Toolbars Used**

View >
Toolbars
and select
Standard and
Formatting.

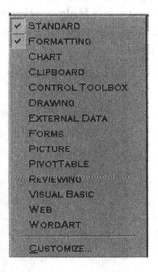

▶ **Help Options/Office Assistant**

Click on **Office Assistant** > Type in a topic or
question, press **Enter/Return** > Click on topic to
learn more.

Turn off Assistant: (WIN) *Right* click > **Hide** or
(MAC) Ctrl + Click > Hide.

Help > **Microsoft Excel Help** also brings up the
help contents.

▶ **Other Information**

WIN: **Ctrl** key = **MAC: Command** ⌘ key.

■ 2

Creating a Gradebook

A ny educator's worst nightmare is to have his or her gradebook lost or stolen. Even if students and parents are understanding, it may be difficult to locate all the graded material and put the gradebook back together. This can be especially difficult near the end of a grading period.

An electronic gradebook, created using Microsoft Excel, may be a solution to this problem. There are many unique features that make creating an electronic gradebook using Microsoft Excel ideal for the classroom:

► An electronic gradebook/spreadsheet is portable. Disks can be taken to the office, classroom, or even used on a home computer.

► Multiple copies can be made as backups, storing one copy in a fireproof safe.

► Gradebooks/spreadsheets can be password protected.

► Gradebooks are simple to set up.

► Entering information and making changes is less complicated.

► Mathematical errors are minimized.

► Gradebooks can be used as databases to keep track of student information. You may not be able to use database features with shareware programs.

▶ Excel can be used to create charts and graphs to simplify student statistics. You may not be able to create charts or graphs with shareware programs.

The Basics of the Program

The first step in creating a gradebook is to understand the component parts. A spreadsheet's component parts form the building blocks of the gradebook. Setting up a gradebook correctly from the start ensures fewer problems in the future. Launching Microsoft Excel automatically launches a new Excel file.

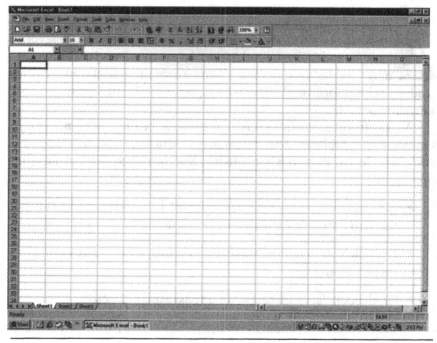

Figure 2.1 Basic Spreadsheet

When you launch Excel, a new "workbook" is created. A workbook is the basic file that stores all of your information.

Each workbook can contain multiple worksheets and chartsheets so that all your information is located in one  place. Think of each workbook as a book and each worksheet (spreadsheet) or chart as the "pages" within a book.

Each worksheet contains basic components that provide the "building blocks" for the gradebook.

The **Current Cell** is the basic building block for the spreadsheet. It can contain either text or numbers and can be formatted in a number of different ways. Each cell is contained within the intersection of a row and a column. Rows are numbered 1 to 65536 and columns are lettered A to IV.

Figure 2.2 Basic Spreadsheet Components

Clicking on the **Column Header** selects an entire column. Clicking on a **Row Header** selects an entire row. You can also complete various resizing tasks using the Headers (see "Changing the Column Width").

The **Name Box** contains the name of the current cell. If you click in the very first cell, the Name Box will contain the Cell Reference "A1" (the "name" of the cell).

The **Formula Bar** contains the information in the current cell. It can be text, numbers, formulas, and functions. Edit information in the current cell by changing the information in the formula bar.

Cell Ranges

A group of cells is called a **range**. 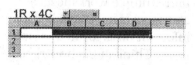 There are many different uses for a range but one of the most common applications is in a formula or function (see Chapter 3). While highlighting the cells in a range, notice that the name box will change to show you the number of rows by the number of columns that you are highlighting. To highlight a range, click on the first cell you would like to include, hold the mouse button down, and drag over to the last cell that you would like to include. When the mouse is released, the name box reverts to the first cell in the range.

Tip: Clicking and dragging is only one way of selecting a range. Another way is to hold down the Shift key as you use the arrow keys to highlight the cells to be included in the range.

Setting Up a Gradebook

The first step in creating a new gradebook is to create a new Excel Workbook.

Launching Excel automatically creates a blank workbook and three blank worksheets. You only need to save the workbook to begin to create your spreadsheet.

Saving

WINDOWS

1. Select **File Menu**, choose **Save As**.

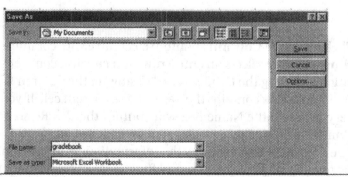

Figure 2.3   Save As—Windows

2. Make sure that the folder name is *My Documents.*

3. Click in the box labeled *File name:* and type "gradebook" (this will be the name of your workbook [file]).

4. Click on the **Save** button.

MACINTOSH

1. Select **File** menu, choose **Save As**.

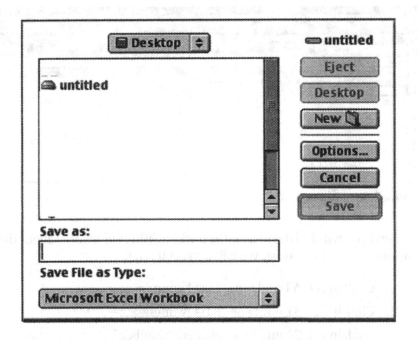

Figure 2.4   Save As—Macintosh

2. Click on the **Desktop** button—you will be saving directly to the desktop.

3. Click in the box labeled *File name:* and type "gradebook" (this will be the name of your workbook [file]).

4. Click on the **Save** button.

Adding Text

Adding text is a simple matter. Click in the cell where you would like to begin entering information and press **Enter/Return** or **Tab** when you are finished. In a spreadsheet, if you press **Enter/Return**, the next cell below the current cell will be selected. **Shift + Return** will move the cursor up one cell. The **Tab** key selects the next cell to the right. To go back to the previous cell after pressing the Tab key, simply hold down the **Shift** key while you press **Tab** again. Finally, the arrow keys can also be used to navigate up, down, left, or right.

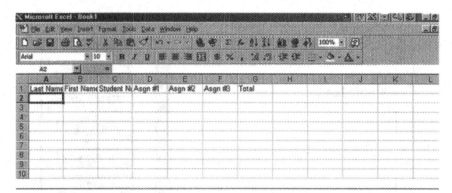

Figure 2.5 Adding Text

Next you will add the text for the basic layout. Don't worry about the column width at this time. We will correct it later.

1. Click in cell A1 and type "Last Name."

2. Click in cell B1 and type "First Name."

3. Click in cell C1 and type "Student Number."

4. Click in cell D1 and type "Asgn #1."

5. Click in cell E1 and type "Asgn #2."

6. Click in cell F1 and type "Asgn #3."

7. Click in cell G1 and type "Total."

Tip: You can also use the **Tab** key or **Right arrow** key to move to the next cell.

Changing the Column Width

To change the column width, you have several options:

1. You can move to the column header between the columns you want to widen and double click. This will "autosize" the columns to fit the text that you have in your column.
2. You can move to the column header between the columns you want to widen and click and drag to manually change the size. The cursor changes to a double-sided arrow. You will see the width (in number of characters) as you drag to the right.
3. You can click on the column header to select the entire column. Then, you can choose **Format > Column > Width** from the pop-up menu. The column width is in number of characters. This is a less often used option but works well if you have a specific width that is necessary or want to make the column widths uniform.

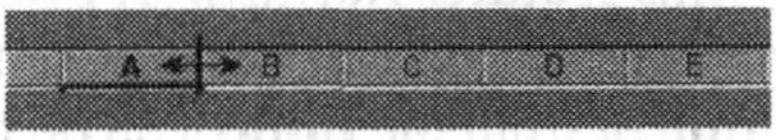

Try each of these methods now to increase the size of columns A, B, and C.

Entering Gradebook Information

Next you will be filling in more cells with the specific sample student information. Leave the total column blank for now.

Add the names and numbers as they appear in Figure 2.6. Notice how the names line up on the left-hand side while the numbers line up

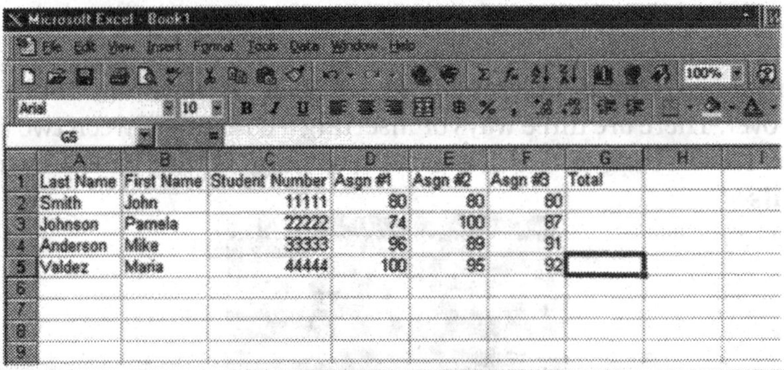

Last Name	First Name	Student Number	Asgn #1	Asgn #2	Asgn #3	Total
Smith	John	11111	80	80	80	
Johnson	Pamela	22222	74	100	87	
Anderson	Mike	33333	96	89	91	
Valdez	Maria	44444	100	95	92	

Figure 2.6 Entering Gradebook Information

on the right-hand side. Also notice that the student numbers also line up on the right-hand side even though we will not be performing mathematical functions with this number.

Freezing Panes

This is an important feature of spreadsheets that will allow you to keep some cell ranges (such as titles, names, etc.) "frozen" (or constant) so that they can be viewed at all times, regardless of scrolling.

Note: It is not a difficult feature to implement. However, where you place your cursor makes all the difference in the proper implementation of this feature. Not to worry—even if you place your cursor in the wrong cell, you can always use the *Undo* feature (either from **Edit > Undo** or from the **Undo** icon on the toolbar).

Look at Figure 2.6. What information would you like to remain constant to view regardless of where you scroll? At first glance, you might think that the column titles across the top are the most critical. However, it is also important for the student names to be viewed as well. With this in mind, it is critical that you place the cursor in cell "C2." All columns to the left of the current cell and all cells above the current cell will remain "frozen" or constant.

Once you have determined the correct cell in which to click, simply choose **Window > Freeze Panes**. Now, if you scroll up, down, left, or right, your titles and other important data do not move.

Inserting Rows, Columns, or Cells

Let's revisit our gradebook example (Figure 2.6).

If we need to add Assignment #4, we need to "move" the Total column over. There are three ways of inserting a column between two columns. The first way is to click in a cell in column "G" and choose **Insert > Cells**.

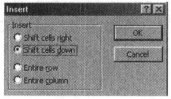

Choosing **Shift cells right**, moves the cell to the right of the current cell. "Shift cells down" will only move the cell beneath the current cell. Choose **Entire column** to insert a column for Assignment #4.

The second option is to click in column "G" and choose **Insert > Columns**. This is a fairly easy method for inserting columns but provides fewer options than **Insert > Cells**.

The easiest method by far is to *right* click (**MAC: Ctrl + Click**) on the column header and choose **Insert** from the pop-up menu:

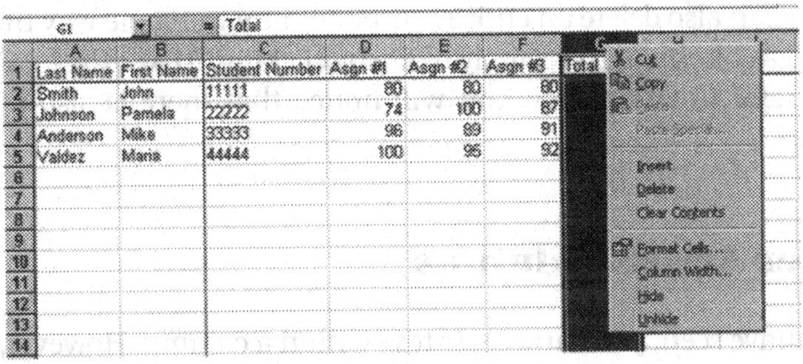

Figure 2.7   Insert—Pop-Up Menu

WINDOWS

Click on the column "G" header with the *right* mouse button. Choose **Insert** from the pop-up menu. Excel automatically inserts a column because an entire column was selected by clicking on the column header. Label your new column "Asgn #4."

MACINTOSH

Hold down the **Control** key and click on the column "G" header with the mouse button. Choose **Insert** from the pop-up menu. Excel automatically inserts a column because an entire column was selected by clicking on the column header. Label your new column "Asgn #4."

Deleting Rows, Columns, or Cells

Deleting information is very similar to inserting information. You will notice that there is no "Delete" menu (like the "Insert" menu). Instead, you will use the delete options under the **Edit** menu. If you have clicked in a single cell, the *Delete* option will take you to a menu identical to the Insert Cells menu.

If you have an entire column or row selected (because you have clicked on a row or column header), the *Delete* option will remove an entire row or column.

You can also delete an entire row or column the same way that you inserted a column or row simply by **right** clicking (**MAC: Ctrl + Click**). If you refer to Figure 2.8, you will notice that there is also a *Delete* option.

Center Across Columns

As you have seen, you can center text within a column. However, there may be times when you would like to center a title *across* columns.

1. First, select the text and the columns over which you would like to center your title. In this case, the title should be centered over columns A through H. You must highlight not only the text with the title to center but also the cells in the columns across which you would like to center your title. A common mistake is only to highlight the text to center.

	A	B	C	D	E	F	G	H	I
1	Student Gradebook								
2									
3	Last Name	First Name	Student Number	Asgn #1	Asgn #2	Asgn #3	Asgn #4	Total	
4	Smith	John	11111	80	80	80			
5	Johnson	Pamela	22222	74	100	87			
6	Anderson	Mike	33333	96	89	91			
7	Valdez	Maria	44444	100	95	92			
8									
9									
10									

Figure 2.8 Center Across Columns—Highlight

2. Once you have highlighted the necessary cells, click on the **Merge and Center** button located on the toolbar.

The cells will be merged, and your title will be centered across columns.

	A	B	C	D	E	F	G	H
1				Student Gradebook				
2								
3	Last Name	First Name	Student Number	Asgn #1	Asgn #2	Asgn #3	Asgn #4	Total
4	Smith	John	11111	80	80	80		
5	Johnson	Pamela	22222	74	100	87		
6	Anderson	Mike	33333	96	89	91		
7	Valdez	Maria	44444	100	95	92		
8								
9								
10								

Figure 2.9   Center Across Columns Example

Formatting Numbers Using the Options in the Toolbar

Occasionally, the default format for numbers is not accurate. For example, if we simply calculate or include numbers without changing the format, it is difficult to tell them apart. Figure 2.17 illustrates this concept.

You will notice that all of the numbers look the same even though they should be formatted differently. The *Total* column automatically rounds the number up,

Total	Percentage	$
320	0.8	1
353	0.8825	2
376	0.94	0.5
377	0.9425	5

without decimals; the percentage column numbers don't look like percentages: and the money column doesn't look a thing like currency.

To make easy and quick formatting changes, simply highlight the cells that you want to change and click on the formatting option that you would like on the toolbar.

Change the Format of a Cell or Range of Cells

1. Click on either the individual cell or (in our case), click on column header "C" to select the entire student number column. Next, click on the **Format** menu and choose **Cells**.

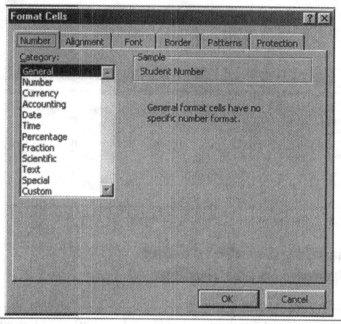

Figure 2.10 Format Cells Dialog Box

2. Notice that there are a number of different options from which to choose. For our purpose, we will change the formatting only for the Student Number.

3. Even though we are dealing with text, you'll notice that the *Text* category is listed under the **Number** tab.

4. Select **Text** to change the format of the student number from *General* to *Text* and click **OK**.

5. Notice that the numbers now line up on the left-hand side.

Format > Cells Options

Number Tab: The Different Types of Number Formatting

▶ **General:** General format cells have no specific number format. This is the default for cell formatting.

▶ **Number:** Number is used for general displays of numbers. With this option, you can specify decimal places, commas, red-and-black color formatting, and parentheses for negative numbers.

▶ **Currency:** Currency formats are used for general monetary values. Like the number-formatting option, you can specify decimal places, red-and-black color formatting, and parentheses for negative numbers.

▶ **Accounting:** Accounting formats line up the currency symbol and decimal points in a column. With this option, decimal places and the symbols can be specified (such as a dollar sign).

▶ **Date:** Date formats display date and time serial numbers as date values. Use time formats to display just the time portion. With this option, there is a variety of date formats from which to choose (e.g., 3/9/05, March 9, 2005).

▶ **Time:** Time formats display date and time serial numbers as time values. Use date formats to display just the date portion. With this option, you have a variety of time formats from which to choose (e.g., 1:30 PM, 13:30).

▶ **Percentage:** Percentage formats multiply the cell value by 100 and display the results with a percentage symbol.

▶ **Fraction:** Fraction formats display the cell value as a fraction. This option provides a variety of fraction formats from which to choose (e.g., by halves, by fourths).

▶ **Scientific:** The scientific format displays numbers in scientific notation. You can specify decimal places with this option.

▶ **Text:** Text format cells are treated as text even when a number is displayed in the cell. The cell is displayed exactly as entered.

▶ **Special:** Special formats are useful for tracking list and database values. Specific formats available in this option are Zip code, Zip code +4, Phone number, and Social Security Number.

► **Custom:** By using the custom format, you can create your own formatting option for repeated use. Using an existing format option as a starting point, you can then name the format and use it repeatedly.

Alignment Tab: Aligning Text and Numbers

There are a number of different options for aligning text. Text and numbers can be formatted horizontally (e.g., Left, Center, Right) or vertically (e.g., Bottom, Center, Top). In addition, the text orientation can be changed (e.g., text rotation to a specified degree), or modified with a variety of text controls (e.g., Wrap text, Shrink to fit, Merge cells).

Font Tab

As with a word processor, you can specify the font, font style (such as bolding or italicizing), font size, underline, color, and effect (such as strikethrough, superscript, or subscript).

Border Tab

The border-formatting section allows you to place a formatted border around a cell or around, through a range of cells, or both. With this option, you can select the parts of the cells to which to add a border (e.g., top, bottom, sides). There are also a number of line styles (such as single, double, and dashed lines). In addition, you can choose a special color for your border.

Patterns Tab

Most often, the pattern feature is used for shading a cell. This can be helpful when trying to add emphasis to or separation for a cell. With this option, there are a variety of colors and patterns from which to choose.

Protection Tab

With this formatting feature, you can either "lock" or "hide" a cell. Locking cells does not allow them to be deleted. This is especially useful in protecting a cell with a complicated formula or function that you do not want to accidentally delete. Hiding cells literally hides the cell from view.

Formatting Rows

Two of the options under the **Format > Rows** menu allow you to change the row height. You can change the row height manually (12.75 is the default) or you can autofit (Excel will select the row height based on the contents of the cells). The other two options allow you to hide and unhide a row. This feature is very helpful if you want to hide certain information from view before printing.

Formatting Columns

Located under **Format > Columns**, many of the features are used to format the width of the column. *Width* and *Standard Width* allow you to manually set the width (8.43 is the default) and set and change the standard width (from 8.43 to another number that you specify). Like the rows, Excel can autofit the column based on its contents. Also, like the rows, you can hide and unhide columns. This feature is very helpful if you want to hide certain information from view before printing.

Naming Sheets

Because there are multiple sheets, it is wise to name your sheets. You can do this one of two ways. You can choose **Format > Sheet > Rename**  to name the current sheet. However, there is an easier method:

Simply double click on the **Sheet** tab that you wish to name. The sheet name will be highlighted (indicating that you can type over it). Your name is limited to 30 characters (including spaces). Go ahead and name the sheet "Quarter 1 Grades."

AutoFormat

AutoFormat applies a preset "style" to a range of cells. You cannot apply an AutoFormat to a single cell. You can choose to apply the AutoFormat for numbers, borders, fonts, patterns, alignment, and width/height (or any combination of these formats).

There are a variety of options from which to choose including simple black and white and very colorful (see Figure 2.11).

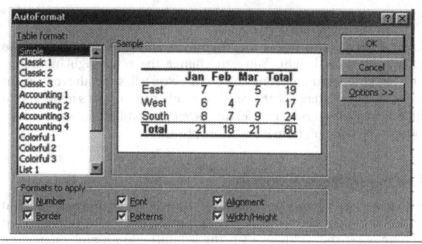

Figure 2.11   AutoFormat Dialog Box

Try the *autoformatting* feature now.

1. Highlight the entire range of cells that you want to autoformat.

2. Choose **Format > AutoFormat**.

3. Scroll through the different options and choose an option that you find appealing.

	A	B	C	D	E	F	G	H
1			Student Gradebook					
2								
3	Last Name	First Name	Student Number	Asgn #1	Asgn #2	Asgn #3	Asgn #4	Total
4	Smith	John	11111	80	80	80	80	320
5	Johnson	Pamela	22222	74	100	87	92	353
6	Anderson	Mike	33333	96	89	91	100	376
7	Valdez	Maria	44444	100	95	92	90	377
8								
9								
10								

Figure 2.12   Example of AutoFormatting

If you decide that you don't like the AutoFormat that you have chosen, you can either choose **Edit > Undo** or choose **Format > AutoFormat** to select another format.

Formatting Styles

To apply several formats in one step and ensure that cells have consistent formatting, you can create and apply a style to the cells. You can create your own combination of styles to apply a font and font size, number formats, and cell borders and shading, and to protect cells from changes.

Try setting up a style now.

1. Click on a blank cell below your data—this will be the cell to which the new style will be applied. It's only for practice purposes.

2. Choose **Format > Style**.

3. In the *Style Name* box, type "Test Style."

4. Click the **Modify** button to add different elements to your style.

5. Click on the **Number** tab and change the *Category* to *Text*.

6. Click on the **Border** tab and change the Border Style to a double-lined outline.

7. Click on the **Add** button and then the **OK** button. The New Style will now be applied.

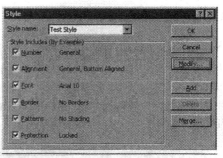

Figure 2.13 Formatting Style Dialog Box

Figure 2.14 Format Cells Dialog Box

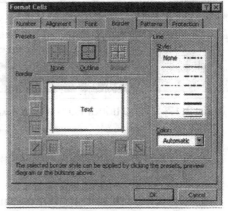

Figure 2.15 Border Dialog Box

Conditional Format

Conditional formatting highlights changing data that you wish to monitor. If data meets the criteria that you set, Excel applies formatting that you specify (such as a specific type of shading). This is a very useful feature if you would like to highlight the names of students who make a specific grade on an assignment.

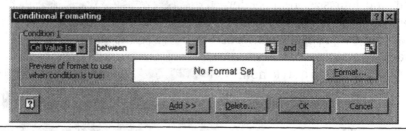

Figure 2.16 Conditional Formatting Dialog Box

To apply a conditional format:

1. Choose **Format > Conditional Format**.

2. In the 3rd box, type "90"; in the 4th box, type "100." The conditional format will automatically be applied to grades of 90 through 100.

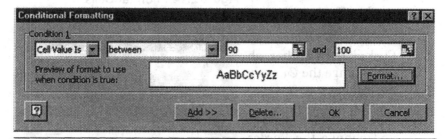

Figure 2.17 Conditional Formatting Example

3. Choose the specific formatting necessary. In this case, choose **Bold**.

4. Click the **OK** button in the format cells followed by the **OK** button in the *Conditional Formatting* box.

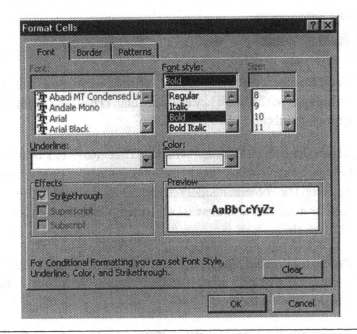

Figure 2.18 Format Cells Example

The bolding format will automatically be applied to any number between 90 and 100 on your entire spreadsheet.

If you no longer want the conditional format to be applied, you can delete it by choosing **Format > Conditional Format** and clicking the **Delete** button. You can then choose the conditional format you want to delete.

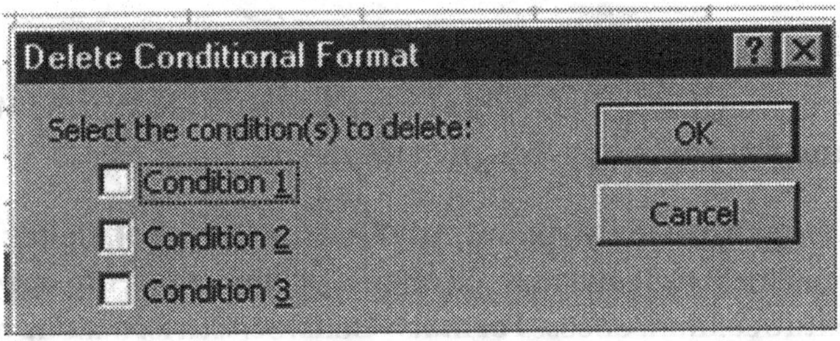

Figure 2.19 Delete Conditional Format Dialog Box

Quick Review

▶ **Cell Ranges:** Click and drag to highlight a group of cells (range) or hold down the **Shift** key and use the **Arrow** keys to highlight a group of cells.

▶ **Changing the Column Width:** Three ways (1) Double click between the column headers to "Autosize," (2) Click and drag between the column headers to resize, or (3) Click on the column header and choose **Format > Column > Width** to choose a specific width.

▶ **Freezing Panes:** Click in the cell to the right and below the information to remain constant, then choose **Window > Freeze Panes**.

▶ **Inserting and/or Deleting Rows, Columns, or Cells:** (1) Click in a cell and choose **Insert > Cells.** Then choose **Entire Column, Row,** or **Shift Cells Left/Right,** (2) Click in a cell and choose **Insert > Column/Row,** or (3) *Right* click (**MAC: Ctrl + Click)** on the column/row header and choose **Insert** from the pop-up menu.

▶ **Deleting Cells, Rows, and Columns:** (1) Click in a cell and choose **Edit > Delete.** Then choose **Entire Column, Row,** or **Shift Cells Left/Right,** or (2) *Right* click (**MAC: Ctrl + Click)** on the column/row header and choose **Delete** from the pop-up menu.

▶ **Centering Across Columns:** Select the text and the columns over which you would like to center your title. Click on the **Merge and Center** button located in the toolbar.

▶ **Changing the Format of Any Cell (or Range of Cells):** Click on either the individual cell or on a column header to select the entire column. Choose **Format > Cells.** Select a formatting option and click **OK**.

▶ **Naming Sheets:** Double click on the sheet name to highlight the default name. Type a new sheet name.

▶ **Using AutoFormat:** Highlight the entire range of cells that you want to AutoFormat. Choose **Format > AutoFormat.** Select an option.

▶ **Using Formatting Styles:** Click on the cell or range of cells to which to apply the style. Choose **Format > Style.** In the *Style Name* box, type a new style name. Click the **Modify** button to add different elements to the style. Click on tabs to choose different elements. Click on the **Add** button and then **OK.**

▶ **Using Conditional Formatting:** Choose **Format > Conditional Format.** Choose the conditions for the formatting. Choose the specific formatting necessary. In this case, choose **Bold** then **OK.**

Basic Math and Excel

O ne of the biggest advantages of using Excel is the ability to convert a series of numbers into an equation or formula quickly and easily. Suppose you want your students to use a spreadsheet for a mathematics lesson, but you're afraid your students know more about spreadsheets than you do.

After launching Excel, you notice the symbols for addition and subtraction are quite obvious—the plus sign for addition is the same. The minus sign is the same symbol as the hyphen. "But what do I use for multiplication and subtraction?" you ask a colleague who has come into the lab. "It's a lot like a calculator," your colleague replies. "Use the asterisk for multiplication. The slash, on the same key as the question mark, is used for division. For raising to a power, you use the caret, usually found above the 6."

Basic Operators

To perform mathematical operations within the spreadsheet, you need to use the correct symbols for the operators. The most common symbols are shown in Figure 3.1.

Operator	Example	Description
+	3 + 5	Adds 3 and 5
–	29 – 13	Subtracts 13 from 29
*	8 * 9	Multiplies 8 and 9
/	25/5	Divides 25 by 5
^	3^2	Raises 3 to the second power or "squares 3"

Figure 3.1   Common Symbols for Operators in a Spreadsheet

You are ready to begin. Say you want to add 35, 98, 79, and 68. Type those numbers into a cell and press the **Enter/Return** key. "Hey, what's wrong? Nothing happened. There's no answer."

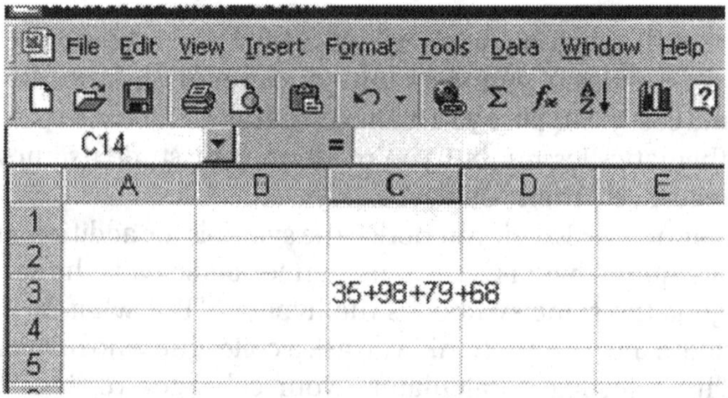

Figure 3.2   Adding Numbers—Incorrect Example

Using the Equal Sign

To perform an operation, an equal sign must be typed at the beginning of the expression, function, or formula.

Now to work on averages. If you want students to find the average of 76, 89, 58, and 62, start with the equal sign, type in the numbers, and then use the slash for divide and type a "4." Then press the **Enter/Return** key. You say in surprise, "What? That can't be right. Why did the spreadsheet give the wrong answer?"

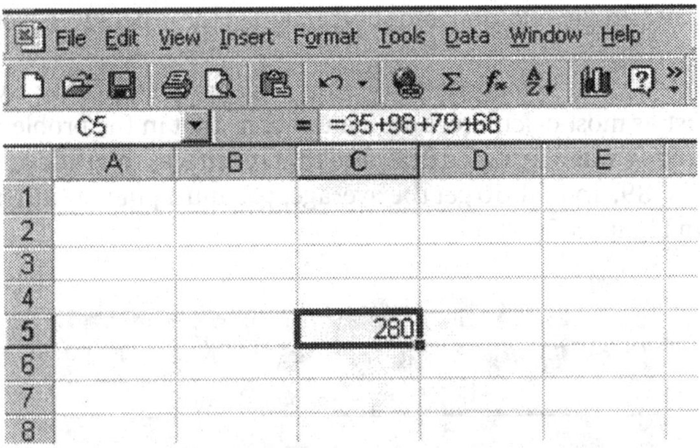

Figure 3.3 Adding Numbers Correctly Using Equal Sign

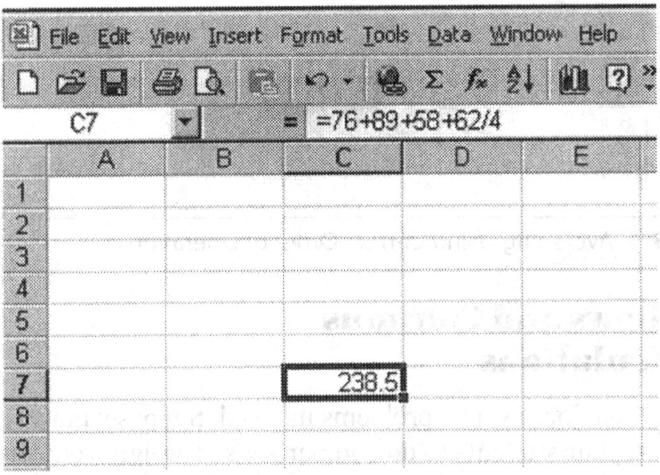

Figure 3.4 Averaging—Incorrect Example

Order of Operations

A spreadsheet calculates a string of mathematical operations using the order of operations. If you remember your junior high mathematics, you probably learned the phrase "Please Excuse My Dear Aunt Sally." That's the mnemonic for the order of operations—parentheses first, exponents next, multiplication and division in the order given from left to right, and finally, addition and subtraction in the order given from left to right.

An electronic spreadsheet uses an Algebraic Operating System (AOS) just as most calculators do. That means that in the problem you entered, 62/4 was calculated first, and that result was then added to the sum of 76, 89, and 58. To get the average, you must put parentheses as shown in Figure 3.5.

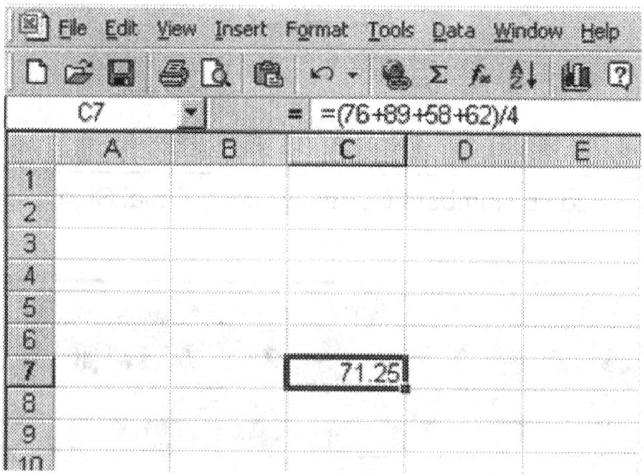

Figure 3.5   Averaging Using Correct Order of Operations

Using Rows and Columns for Calculations

You have been doing single problems in a cell. Suppose, however, that you wanted your students to do comparisons of weights on earth, the moon, and other planets. It would be easier for students to read and interpret the results if everything was laid out in a neat table. After students have looked up the gravity of other planets and the moon as compared to the earth, create the following layout for them to follow (Figure 3.6):

1. Type the spreadsheet title in cell B1. Format it as you learned in the following way:
   a. Highlight cells B1 through F2.
   b. **Select Format > Cells**. Click on the **Alignment** tab, and check *Merge Cells*.

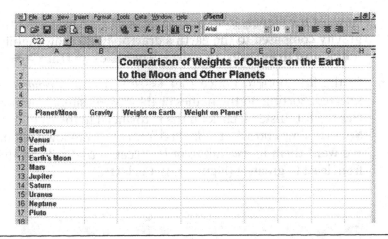

Figure 3.6 Spreadsheet Layout

    c. Type in "Comparison of Weights of Objects on the Earth to the Moon and Other Planets" and format it using font size 14 and bold.

2. Type the column headings in cells A3, A4, and A5.

3. Type the names of the planets and the earth's moon in column A, beginning with cell A8.

4. Type the data for the comparative weight (gravity) for each of the planets and the moon in column B, beginning with cell B8, from the Figure 3.7.

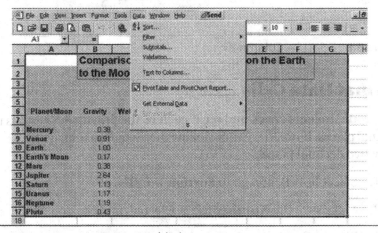

Figure 3.7 Sorting Data—Highlighting

5. Now list the planets from least to greatest with respect to their gravity compared to the earth's gravity. To do that, highlight (**click and drag**) cells A8 to B17. Then click on **Data > Sort**.

6. In the first option, notice that *Column A* and *Ascending* are selected. Sorting on the names of the planets simply alphabetizes the list. Instead, click on the arrowhead to the right of the **Sort** window and select *Column B* from the drop-down options. We want them in ascending order because that will list them from least to greatest (Figure 3.8). Click **OK**.

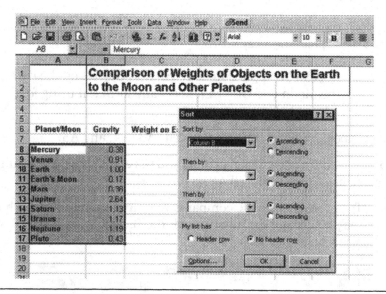

Figure 3.8   Sort by Column B

Format Data Cells

Have your students check and see if each of the gravity figures has two decimal places. If not, have them follow these steps so that all the figures show two decimal places.

1. Select Row B, and go to **Format > Cells**.

2. Make sure the **Number** tab is selected, and click on *Number*.

3. Be sure that it says 2 decimal places and click **OK**.

Copying Data

Let's say that you want to know how much an object that weighs 125 pounds on earth will weigh on each of the other planets and on the moon. Type "125" in cell C8 and copy it into cells C9 through C17. To do that,

1. Click in cell C8 so that it is outlined in black.

2. Move the cursor to the lower right corner of the cell until it turns into a black cross or plus sign.

3. Click and drag the cursor down to C17.

Now it is time to type the formula to compare the weight of a 125-pound object on earth to its weight on the earth's moon. You could type "=0.17*125" in cell D8 and press **Enter/Return**. That would give you the answer for the weight of an object on the moon that weighs 125 pounds on earth. However, that means you would have to type in the formula for each of the planets. If you changed the weight of the object on earth, you would have to change every formula you had typed in column D.

Using Relative References

It is easier to take advantage of the power of the spreadsheet. Instead of typing in each value, use the cell addresses in the formula.

1. Type the formula for the moon's gravity comparison, "=B8*C8" into cell D8. You just learned how to copy from one cell to another. Here's an opportunity to practice that again.

2. Click on cell D8, put the cursor in the lower right-hand corner of the cell until it becomes a black cross and then click and drag down to and including cell D17. The spreadsheet automatically adjusts the cell address as it copies the formula into each of the cells. This is known as a "relative" reference to a cell. You will learn about "absolute" references in the next chapter.

3. Center the data by highlighting cells B8 through D17 and clicking on the **Center Alignment** button in the toolbar.

	A	B	C	D	E	F
1		Comparison of Weights of Objects on the Earth				
2		to the Moon and Other Planets				
3						
4						
5						
6	Planet/Moon	Gravity	Weight on Earth	Weight on Planet		
7						
8	Earth's Moon	0.17	125	21.25		
9	Mercury	0.38	125	47.50		
10	Mars	0.38	125	47.50		
11	Pluto	0.43	125	53.75		
12	Venus	0.91	125	113.75		
13	Earth	1.00	125	125.00		
14	Saturn	1.13	125	141.25		
15	Uranus	1.17	125	146.25		
16	Neptune	1.19	125	148.75		
17	Jupiter	2.64	125	330.00		
18						

Figure 3.9   Centering Data

"What If" Scenario

Now you and your students are ready to do the "What If" use of the spreadsheet. What if the weight of the object on earth was 290 pounds? Change the value in cell C8. Did you notice that the value in cell D8 automatically changed? That is an example of the automatic recalculation that the spreadsheet does when you change a value that is part of a formula.

Manually Recalculating Values

You can disable that feature and manually recalculate the values. To do this,

1. Select **Tools > Options**.

2. From the dialog box, click on the **Calculation** tab.

3. Select the *Manual Calc.* radio button. Notice that there is a **Calc Now (F9)** button. Instead of coming back to this dialog box, simply press **F9** whenever you are ready to recalculate the values. The other selected option is *Recalculate before save.* If you have not recalculated the data before you save your work, the program will recalculate it automatically.

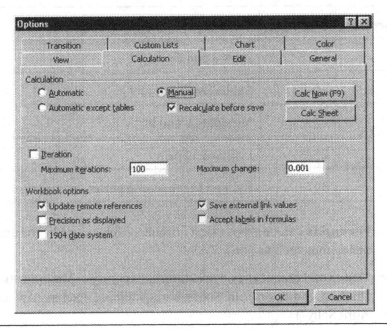

Figure 3.10 Manually Recalculating Values

Now, let's finish this step.

4. Copy the new weight (290) into cells C9 through C17. Notice that this time the data in row D did not change.

5. Press **F9.** (You do not have to highlight row D or even click in one of the cells in row D.)

Normally you would use the manual recalculation option when you have a large spreadsheet. The automatic recalculation of large amounts of data can perceptibly slow down your work. The spreadsheets that we are working with are small enough that the recalculation seems to be instantaneous.

Quick Review

In this chapter, you have learned the basic steps for performing mathematical calculations using a spreadsheet.

▶ **Operators**

Operator	Example	Description
+	3 + 5	Adds 3 and 5
–	29 – 13	Subtracts 13 from 29
*	8 * 9	Multiplies 8 and 9
/	25/5	Divides 25 by 5
^	3^2	Raises 3 to the second power or "squares 3"

▶ **Formulas** can be typed using numbers such as "=5*9" or using cell names such as "=C17*A9."

▶ **Order of Operations:** Parentheses, Exponents, Multiplication, Division, Addition and Subtraction ("Please Excuse My Dear Aunt Sally")

▶ **Using Rows and Columns to Sort Information:** Use the Data > Sort menu option.

▶ **Manually Recalculating Values:** Select Tools > Options. Calculation tab > Manual Calc. radio button. Then press F9 for calculations.

4

Formulas and Functions

*I*n Chapter 3, you learned how to use a formula in a spreadsheet. In this chapter, you will learn to use the Paste Function. The Paste Function will enable you to type common—and not so common—formulas in spreadsheets quickly and easily. Microsoft Excel provides built-in functions for many of the common mathematical calculations in arithmetic, statistics, and accounting that can be used in the classroom.

Let's suppose you are preparing to do a problem-solving activity with your students. You want to incorporate the use of a spreadsheet. The problem asks the students to determine the average number of M&M's in a fun-size package of M&M's. In addition, the students will determine the average number of each color in the package. You have decided that the students will work in groups of four, and then the work of the seven groups will be combined. You want two spreadsheets prepared—one for the small groups and one for the total class.

Setting Up a Spreadsheet

Open a new workbook by going to **File > New** or by pressing the **New Document** icon. First, let's rename the sheets in the spreadsheet. In the lower left hand corner of your screen, right click (**MAC: Ctrl +**

Click) on Sheet 1 and select **Rename** from the drop-down menu. Type in "Group 1." Repeat for Sheet 2 and name that "Class Results."

	A	B	C	D	E	F	G	H	I
1									
2		**M&M's**							
3									
4	Name	Red	Green	Blue	Brown	Orange	Yellow	Total	Average
5	Jo								
6	Bob								
7	Stan								
8	Maria								
9									
10	Total								
11	Average								
12									

Figure 4.1   Small Group Spreadsheet

The small group spreadsheet will look like the above graphic:

1. Create the title and labels for small group worksheets.
   a. Type "M&M's" in cell B2. Change the font size to 14 and bold it. Enlarge the width of the cell to fit the text.
   b. Beginning in cell A4, type the following in row 4: "Name, Red, Green, Blue, Brown, Orange, Yellow, Total, Average"
   c. Beginning in cell A5, type the following in column A: "Jo, Bob, Stan, Maria." In cell A10, type "Total."

The total class worksheet will look like Figure 4.2.

2. Create the title and labels for the class results worksheet.
   a. Click on the **Class Results** tab.
   b. Type "M&M's" in cell B2. Change the font size to 14 and bold it. Enlarge the width of the cell to fit the text.
   c. Beginning in cell A3, type the following in row 3: "Group, Red, Green, Blue, Brown, Orange, Yellow, Total, Average."
   d. Beginning in cell A4, type the following in column A: "Group 1, Group 2, Group 3, Group 4, Group 5, Group 6, Group 7." In cell A12, type "Total" and in cell A13 "Average."

3. Save your workbook as "mandms."

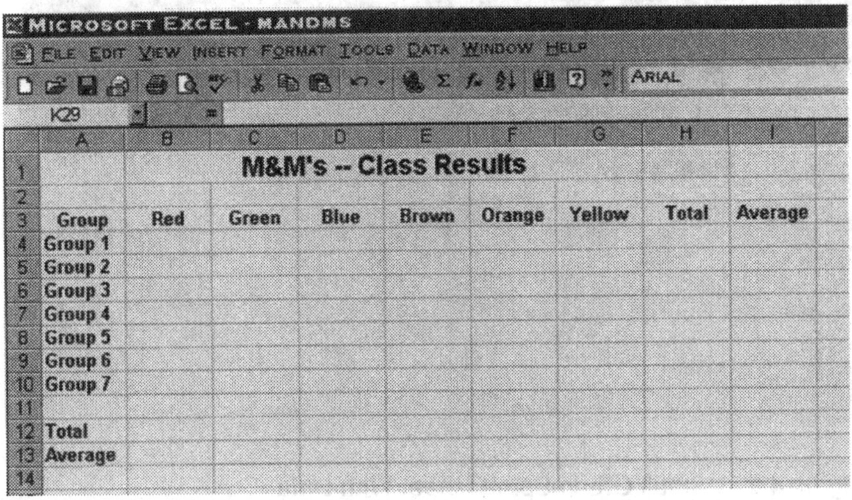

Figure 4.2   Total Class Worksheet

Using Functions

You are going to have the students use two of the functions for this spreadsheet—the Sum( ) function and the Average( ). Notice that function names always end with parentheses. A function accepts or uses zero or more arguments. An argument is the data that will be used in the calculation. It may be described as a range of cells, actual data, or specific cells. For instance, in the function Sum(25, 39, 76) 25, 39, and 76 are the arguments—the numbers or data to be added. In the function Sum(A7:A18), the arguments are the data in all the cells from A7 through A18. In the function Sum(A7, A12, A49), the arguments are the data in those three specific cells. The arguments indicate the data that is to be used in the function. If there are two or more discrete arguments, they are separated with commas. A range of cells in the argument is indicated with a colon. Let's look at the spreadsheet for the small group and see how this works.

The Sum( ) Function

Suppose that Jo, Bob, Stan, and Maria (four of your students) have opened their packages and counted the following numbers of each color.

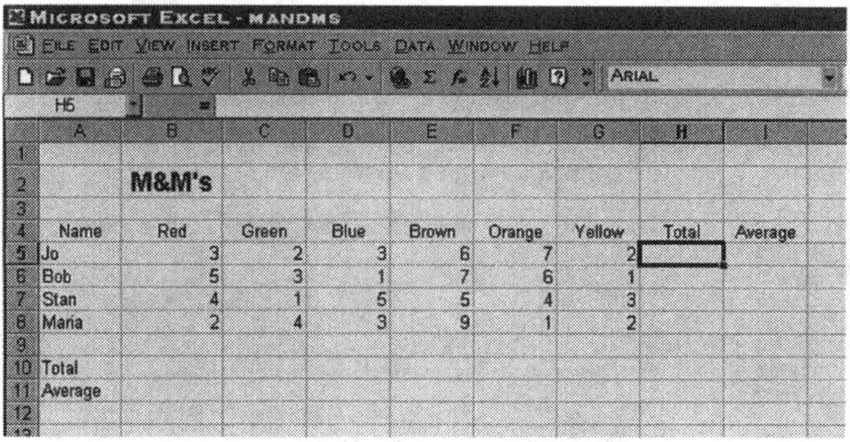

Figure 4.3   Small Group Spreadsheet With Data

1. Click on the *Group 1* tab on the bottom left corner. Input the data as shown in the spreadsheet. You want the students to calculate the total (sum) of each color and the total of each package. The **AutoSum function** is indicated by the large capital E (the Greek letter Σ) found in the toolbar. Be sure that you have clicked on the cell where you want the function to be—in this case H5.

2. Click on cell H5 in this worksheet (Group 1). When you click on the Σ (AutoSum) function, the row or column of data that the spreadsheet assumes you want to sum is indicated with a "running" border of dashes, and the selected cells are shown as a range inside the parentheses in the Formula bar. The Autosum =SUM(B5:G5) adds the values of the cells B7 through G7, Jo's total number of M&M's. If the range is correct, press **Enter/Return** (see Figure 4.4).

3. Click on the Σ (AutoSum) icon in the toolbar. Check to make sure that the range of cells is correct (B5 through G5) in the formula bar and press **Enter/Return**.

What if the range of cells is not correct? The easiest way to correct that is to click in the formula bar and change the range there. Two things to remember: Be sure the closing parenthesis is there. Press **Enter/Return** to exit the formula.

	A	B	C	D	E	F	G	H	I
1									
2		M&M's							
3									
4	Name	Red	Green	Blue	Brown	Orange	Yellow	Total	Average
5	Jo	3	2	3	6	7	2	=SUM(B5:G5)	
6	Bob	5	3	1	7	6	1		
7	Stan	4	1	5	5	4	3		
8	Maria	2	4	3	9	1	2		
9									
10	Total								
11	Average								
12									

Figure 4.4   Autosum Jo's Data

It is important that you press the **Enter/Return** key. A common mistake is to press one of the arrow keys or the Tab key—that simply adds a new cell to the function. Always press **Enter/Return** to leave the cell when you are creating a formula or using a function.

4. Copy the formula into cells H6 through H8 (see Chapter 3). Let's use the AutoSum function again—this time to sum the columns. Notice that there is a blank row between the last data row and the total row. That empty cell (B9) is included in the range. You can edit that in the Formula bar.

5. Click on cell B10.

6. Press on Σ in the toolbar. Correct the range of cells (B5:B9) by changing B9 in the Formula bar to B8. Press **Enter/Return**.

7. Copy the formula into cells C10 through H10.

The Average( ) Function

Now you are ready to type the Average( ) function. Next to the AutoSum icon in the toolbar is the mathematical symbol for a function (*fx*).

1. Click on the cell that you want to put the formula in first (cell I5 in the *Group 1* worksheet).

	A	B	C	D	E	F	G	H	I
1									
2		M&M's							
3									
4	Name	Red	Green	Blue	Brown	Orange	Yellow	Total	Average
5	Jo	3	2	3	6	7	2	23	
6	Bob	5	3	1	7	6	1	23	
7	Stan	4	1	5	5	4	3	22	
8	Maria	2	4	3	9	1	2	21	
9									
10	Total	=SUM(B5:B9)							
11	Average								
12									

Figure 4.5   AutoSum Total for Red M&M's

	A	B	C	D	E	F	G	H	I
1									
2		M&M's							
3									
4	Name	Red	Green	Blue	Brown	Orange	Yellow	Total	Average
5	Jo	3	2	3	6	7	2	23	
6	Bob	5	3	1	7	6	1	23	
7	Stan	4	1	6	5	4	3	22	
8	Maria	2	4	3	9	1	2	21	
9									
10	Total	=SUM(B5:B8)							
11	Average								
12									

Figure 4.6   AutoSum Correction

2. Now, click on the **Function** icon (*fx*). The *Paste Function* dialog box comes up with two columns. On the left is the list of categories of functions. On the right are the functions in that category.

3. Select *Average* if it is in the list on the right of *Most Recently Used functions* and press **OK** to bring up the *Average* dialog box. Again click **OK**.

If Average( ) is not in the list of *Most Recently Used functions*, click on *Statistical* in the list on the left and then select AVERAGE.

Because there is a Total column between the last data cell (G5) and the cell selected for the Average function, that "extra" cell shows up in

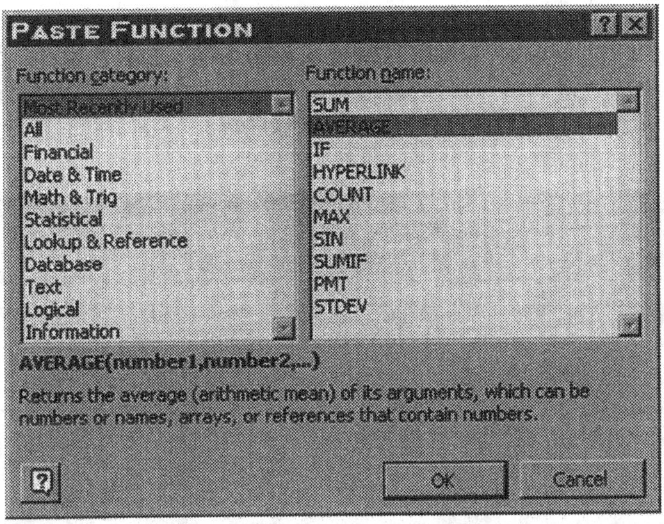

Figure 4.7   Paste Function—Average

the range. You can edit that now in the *Average* dialog box and change
the H5 to G5.

In the range of cells shown, change H5 to G5 and then press
Enter/Return. You may want to format the cells so that the numbers
display only one or two decimal places. See Chapter 2 to review the
directions for doing that.

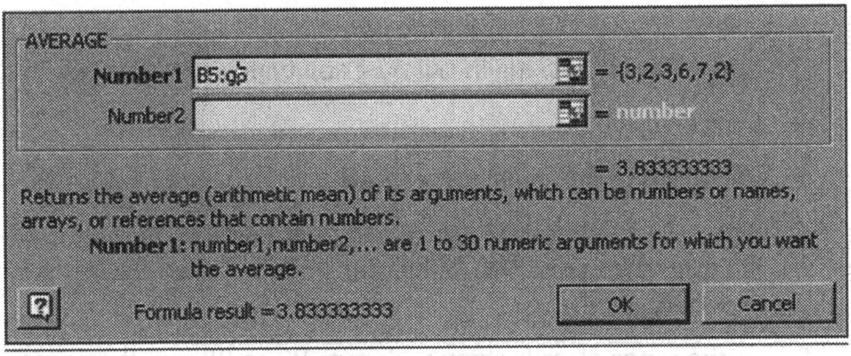

Figure 4.8   Average Dialog Box

4.   Now copy that formula into cells I6 through I10.

Notice that in cell H10 there is a something you have not seen
before: #DIV/0!

You are being told that you are doing a "no-no"—trying to divide by zero. Because row H is to be a blank row, simply clear that cell. One way to do that is to click in that cell and then press either the **Backspace** or **Delete** key.

	A	B	C	D	E	F	G	H	I
1									
2		**M&M's**							
3									
4	Name	Red	Green	Blue	Brown	Orange	Yellow	Total	Average
5	Jo	3	2	3	6	7	2	23	4
6	Bob	5	3	1	7	6	1	23	4
7	Stan	4	1	5	5	4	3	22	4
8	Maria	2	4	3	9	1	2	21	4
9									#DIV/0!
10	Total	14	10	12	27	18	8	89	15
11	Average								
12									

Figure 4.9 Divided by Zero Error Message

5. Clear cell H10 because that also is to be blank.

   The small group spreadsheet is nearly completed. Each individual package has been summed and averaged. Now the total of each color and the total of all the packages must be averaged. Again, the Average( ) function will be used.

   Add a label by clicking in cell A11 and typing in "Averages."

6. Click on cell B11.

7. Click on *fx* in the toolbar to get the **Paste Function** dialog box.

8. Select *Average* from the list on the right of *Most Recently Used functions* then press **OK**. When the *Average* dialog box appears, press **OK** again.

9. In the range of cells shown, change B9 to B8 and then press **Enter/Return**.

10. Copy this formula into cells C11 through H11.

11. Clear cell H10 because we want that one to be blank.

MICROSOFT EXCEL - MANDMS

FILE EDIT VIEW INSERT FORMAT TOOLS DATA WINDOW HELP

H11   = =AVERAGE(H5:H8)

	A	B	C	D	E	F	G	H	I
1									
2		M&M's							
3									
4	Name	Red	Green	Blue	Brown	Orange	Yellow	Total	Average
5	Jo	3	2	3	6	7	2	23	4
6	Bob	5	3	1	7	6	1	23	4
7	Stan	4	1	5	5	4	3	22	4
8	Maria	2	4	3	9	1	2	21	4
9									#DIV/0!
10	Total	14	10	12	27	18	8	89	15
11	Average	4	3	3	7	5	2	22	
12									

Figure 4.10 Total Average

Using Paste Special

Using a Class Spreadsheet in the One-Computer Classroom

What if there is only one computer in your classroom? Your students can type their data on separate sheets in the workbook. Their results can be linked to the class spreadsheet. Any changes in the student worksheets will automatically be reflected in the class results.

Let's walk through that process with just one group for now. What you want in the class worksheet are the totals for each group. So, for the group that you have been working with,

1. Select cells B10 through G10.

2. Using either **Ctrl + C (MAC: ⌘ + C)** or **Copy** from the **Edit** menu, copy those cells.

3. Open the class worksheet (Class Results) and select cells B4 through G4.

4. Select **Edit** and select **Paste Special** to bring up the *Paste Special* dialog box.

5. Near the bottom is a button labeled **Paste Link**. Click on that.

6. If the data were available, repeat this process for each small group, selecting B5 through G5 for Group 2, B6 through G6 for Group 3, and so on.

7. Save your work.

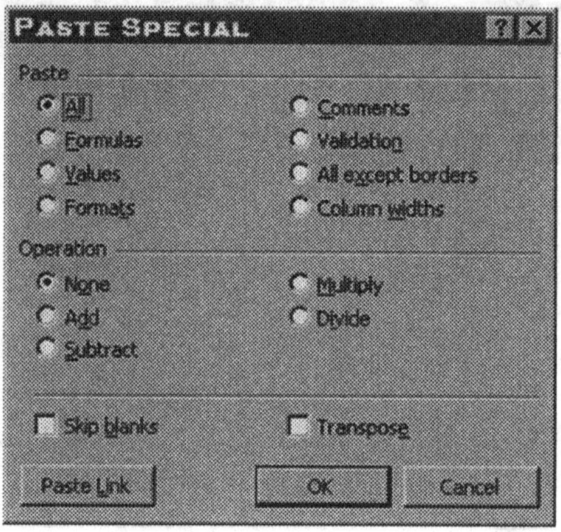

Figure 4.11 Paste Special Dialog Box

You will see that the totals for each color of M&M's for Group 1 have been copied. Now, if you go back to the data that Group 1 has recorded and change some of the numbers, you will see those changes reflected in the class worksheet.

For example, if on Sheet 1 you change Jo's number of red M&M's from 3 to 8 then click out of the cell, the total number of red M&M's changes from 14 to 19 for the group. The second worksheet (class) total for red M&M's also changes to 19 automatically. Select **Edit > Undo** to revert back to 3 red M&M's and 14 total reds on both worksheets.

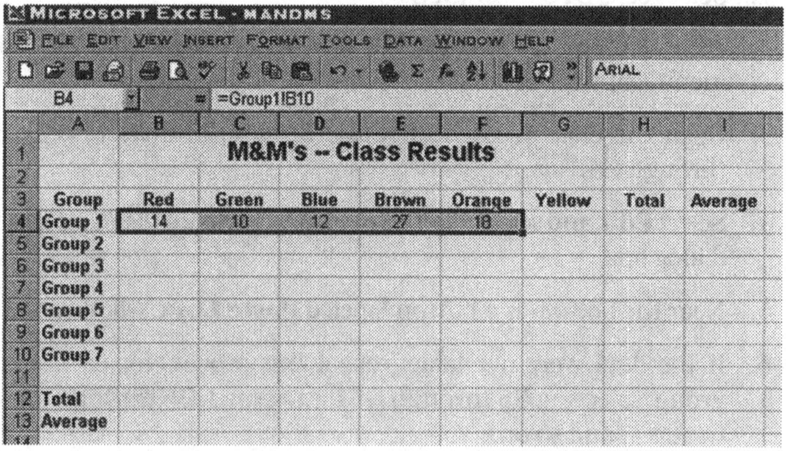

Figure 4.12 Copied Totals From Group 1

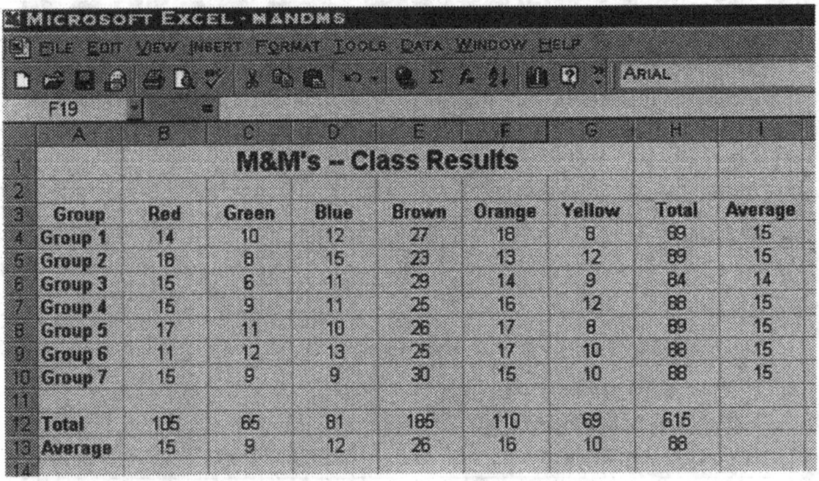

MICROSOFT EXCEL - MANDMS

	A	B	C	D	E	F	G	H	I
1	M&M's -- Class Results								
2									
3	Group	Red	Green	Blue	Brown	Orange	Yellow	Total	Average
4	Group 1	14	10	12	27	18	8	89	15
5	Group 2	18	8	15	23	13	12	89	15
6	Group 3	15	6	11	29	14	9	84	14
7	Group 4	15	9	11	25	16	12	88	15
8	Group 5	17	11	10	26	17	8	89	15
9	Group 6	11	12	13	25	17	10	88	15
10	Group 7	15	9	9	30	15	10	88	15
11									
12	Total	105	65	81	185	110	69	615	
13	Average	15	9	12	26	16	10	88	

Figure 4.13 Class Results

Absolute and Relative Addresses

So far, in Chapters 2 and 3, you have seen examples of "relative addressing"—in other words, the cell addresses were changed when the formulas or functions were copied into other cells. You are going to use a spreadsheet in a problem-solving class that requires the use of an absolute cell address.

Estimating Reasonable Quotient Spreadsheet

The following spreadsheet is an example of one a teacher might create for teaching a concept or providing practice in a new skill. It is not one that students would normally create —unless the assignment was for a high school mathematics class to demonstrate an understanding of the concept by creating a spreadsheet that could be used by younger students.

For our purposes, you have created this spreadsheet for your class and have met them in the computer lab. A spreadsheet has been created for the students that is designed to engage them in developing their skills in estimating reasonable quotients. When the students open the file "estquo1," the spreadsheet looks like Figure 4.14.

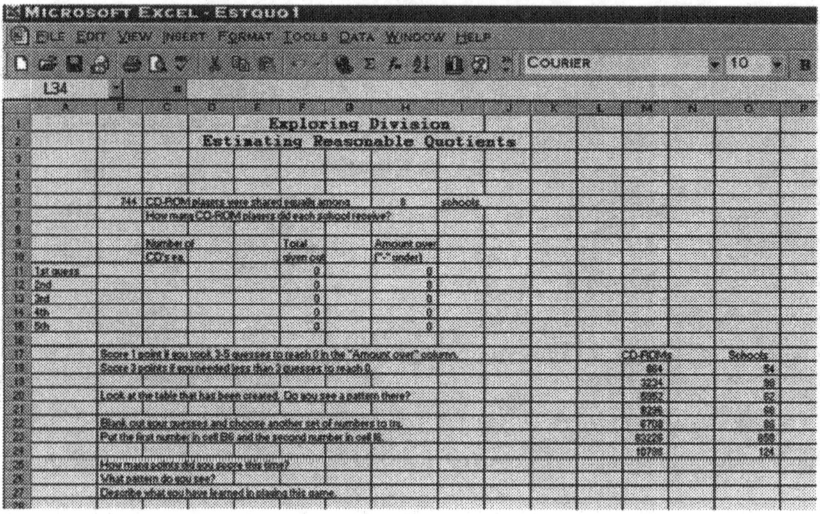

Figure 4.14 Esquo1 Spreadsheet

Create the Estquo1 Spreadsheet

A. Creating Title and Labels for Estimating Quotients Worksheet
    1. Highlight cells E1 through I11.
    2. Select **Format > Cells**. Click on the **Alignment** tab and check *Merge Cells*.
    3. Type in "Exploring Division" and format it using font size 14 and bold.
    4. Highlight cells D2 through J2.
    5. Repeat step 2.
    6. Type in "Estimating Reasonable Quotients" and format it using font size 14 and bold.
    7. In cell B6, type "744." Change the font color to blue.
    8. Highlight cells C6 through G6 and merge the cells.
    9. In cell H6, type "8." Change the font color to blue and center the data.
    10. In cell I6, type "schools."
    11. Highlight cells C7 through H7, merge the cells, and type "How many CD-ROM players did each school receive?"
    12. In cell C9, type "Number of"; in cell F9 type "Total"; and in cell H9 type "Amount over."

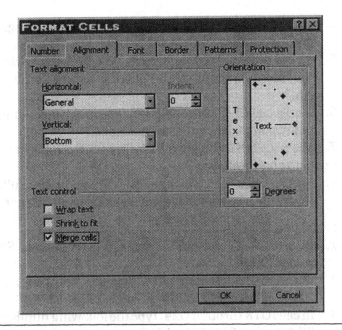

Figure 4.15 Format Cells Dialog Box

13. In cell C10, type "CD's ea."; in cell F10, type "given out"; and in cell H10, type "("-" under)."
14. In cells A11 through A15, type "1st guess," "2nd," "3rd," "4th," and "5th" respectively.

B. Typing the IF Formula Using Absolute Addresses
    1. In cell F11, type the formula, "=IF(C11,C11*H6,0)."
    2. Copy that formula into cells F12 through F15.
    3. In cell H11, type the formula "=B6-F11."
    4. Copy that formula into cells H12 through H15.

C. Finishing the Spreadsheet
    1. Merge cells B17 through I17. Type in the following: "Score 1 point if you took 3 to 5 guesses to reach 0 in the amount over column."
    2. Merge cells B18 through H18. Type in the following: "Score 3 points if you needed less than 3 guesses to reach 0."
    3. Merge cells B20 through H20. Type in the following: "Look at the table that has been created. Do you see a pattern there?"

4. Merge cells B22 through H22. Type in the following: "Blank out your guesses and choose another set of numbers to try."
5. Merge cells B23 through H23. Type in the following: "Put the first number in cell B6 and the second number in cell H6."
6. Merge cells B25 through F25. Type in the following: "How many points did you score this time?"
7. Merge cells B26 through D26. Type in the following: "What patterns do you see?"
8. Merge cells B27 through G27. Type in the following: "Describe what you have learned in playing this game."

D. Providing Additional Sets of Numbers for Practice
1. In cells M17 and O17, type "CD-ROMS" and "Schools" respectively.
2. In cells M18 through M24, type the following numbers: "864, 3234, 5952, 8296, 6708, 90226, 10788."
3. In cells O18 through O24, type the following numbers: "54, 98,62, 68, 86, 858, 124."

Conditional Statements and Absolute Addresses

Let's spend some time looking at the steps that have been taken in creating this spreadsheet. The focus here is on two new ideas: "IF" or conditional statements and absolute addresses. Briefly, here's how the spreadsheet works:

1. Estimate the quotient of 744 divided by 8.

2. In cell C11, type the first estimate.

3. The amount given out and the amount remaining will automatically be calculated in cells F11 and H11.

4. If the value in H11 is not zero, type a new estimate in C12.

5. The goal is to arrive at an exact number given out within five (5) guesses.

Here's what is involved in making Step 3 happen. In F11, you want the product of the estimate times 8 (the value in cell H6) if there is an estimate in C11. If no estimate has been made, you want a zero in the "Total given out" and "Amount over ("−" under) cells. This is often

referred to as a conditional statement. Open the **Paste Function (fx)**.
If the IF function is not in the *Most Recently Used list* of functions, click
on *Logical* from the list of functions on the left. Click on *IF*.

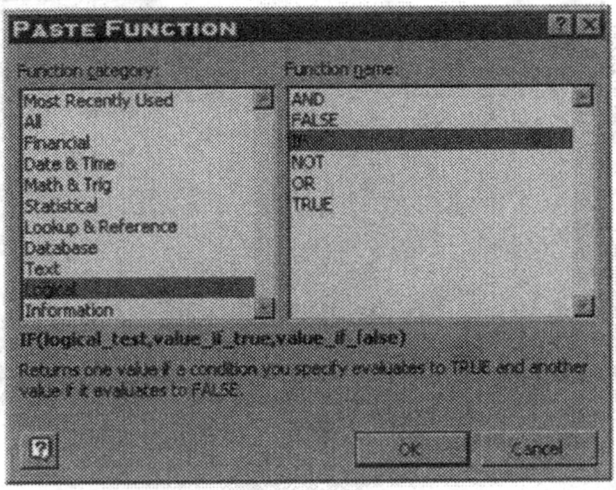

Figure 4.16 Paste Function Dialog Box

The first argument is "logical test." The "logical test" is whether or
not there is a value in cell C11. The "value_if_true"—that is, if there is a
value in cell C11—argument is the product of the number in C11 and
the value in H6. We know from the previous chapter that we can write
that as "C11*H6."

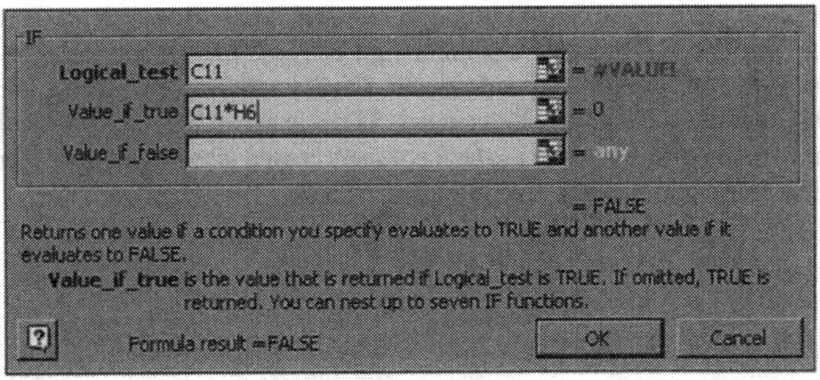

Figure 4.17 Logical Test and Value_If_True

The final argument is the "value_if_false"—that is, if there is no value in cell C1—you have specified that that will be 0.

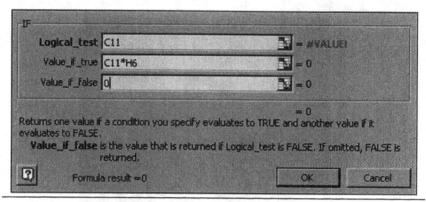

Figure 4.18 Value_If_False

So, the IF function will look like this: "=IF(C11,C11*H6,0)."

So far, so good. But look at what happens when you copy that function into cells F12 through F15. H6 becomes H12, H13, H14, and H15 in each of the succeeding cells.

What happened? H6 is a relative cell address—the spreadsheet assumes that as you copy the formula into other cells, the cell names should change. It's okay that C11 becomes C12, C13, C14, and C15 because that's the cell being considered as students type additional guesses. But the value you're multiplying by—the number of schools— remains unchanged. In other words, we need an absolute cell address. The way we do that is to put a dollar sign in front of the letter and number that make up the cell address. So, H6 is a relative cell address and will change as the formula is copied. H6 is an absolute cell address and will remain the same as the formula is copied (see Figure 4.3). The IF function you need for this spreadsheet is:

$$=IF(C11,C11*\$H\$6,0)$$

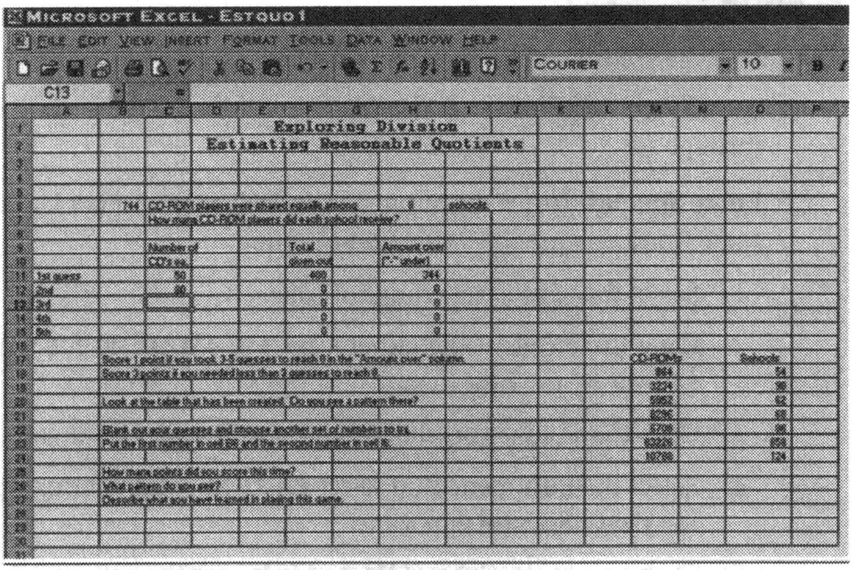

Figure 4.19 Incorrect Relative Cell Address

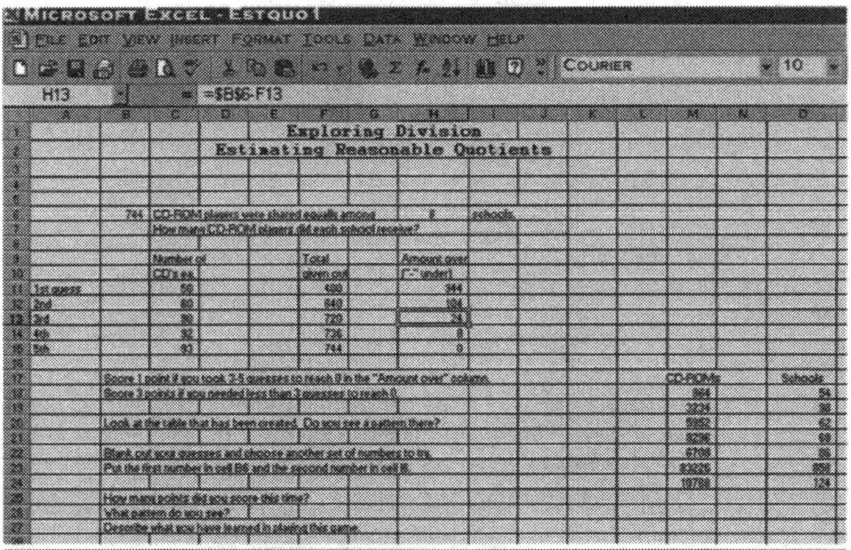

Figure 4.20 Correct Relative Cell Address

Quick Review

▶ **AutoSum:** "=SUM(B5:G5)" adds the values of the cells B5 through G5.

▶ **Paste Special:** To link data from one worksheet to another in the same workbook use the Paste Special option.

1. Select the appropriate range of cells.

2. Copy these cells using either **Ctrl + C (MAC: ⌘ + C)** or **Copy** from the **Edit** menu.

3. Open the desired worksheet and select the appropriate cells.

4. Select the **Edit** menu and select **Paste Special** to bring up the **Paste Special** dialog box.

5. Click on a button labeled **Paste Link** near the bottom.

▶ **Absolute Cell Address:** Put a dollar sign in front of the letter and number that make up the cell address; for example, H6.

⊠ 5

Using Excel as a Database

J ean is a fifth-grade teacher. Currently, Jean's students are preparing for a science fair and are studying photosynthesis and how different factors affect plant growth. At a recent teacher inservice training session, Jean discovered how using the database functions within a spreadsheet might be a great way of helping her students keep track of their data.

► Once set up, databases can be easy to use.

► Databases are searchable—you can find specific data quickly.

► Databases can be searched by specific criteria specified by either the teacher or student.

► Databases can be sorted by a number of different criteria specified by either the teacher or student.

Jean decided to use common philodendron houseplants for the experiments. Students would be assigned to one of nine experimental groups (grown in water, grown in soil, grown without water or soil, grown with recommended amount of fertilizer, grown with too much fertilizer, grown without fertilizer, grown with a grow light/in a window, grown with classroom light, grown in the dark or with a leaf covered).

Jean set up the database for her students. They would use the database to input information such as plant growth, number of yellow leaves, leaf loss, length of brown tips (if any) on the leaves, onset of drooping, and so on. You should set up your spreadsheet/database so it looks as follows:

	A	B	C	D	E	F
1			Plant Growth Experiment			
2	Experimental Group	Growth Wk 1	# Yellow Leaves Wk 1	# Leaves Lost Wk 1	Length of Brown Tips Wk 1	Drooping? Wk 1
3	Water					
4	Soil					
5	None					
6	Normal Fertilizer					
7	Excess Fertilizer					
8	No Fertilizer					
9	Light					
10	Moderate Light					
11	No Light					

Figure 5.1   Basic Photosynthesis Database

Jean also decided to set up separate worksheets for each of the weeks of the experiment. To make sure that there was no confusion, she also set up column labels with the week number as well.

Using "Forms" to Input Information

A data form is a simple method of entering or displaying one row of information at a time in your spreadsheet. Forms require that you have column labels set up so that Excel can create "fields" for the data form. (Note: Data forms can display a maximum of 32 fields at one time.) If you do not have column labels set up and selected, you will receive an error message stating that Microsoft Excel cannot determine which row in your list contains these data labels.

Once you have your data labels set up and selected, get into "Form Mode" simply by choosing **Data > Form** (Figure 5.2).

Notice that the first "field" is the name of the experimental group (in this case, water). From the form, a student can enter the specific information just from his or her group. In addition, there are other features (buttons) on the right-hand side of the form. These buttons and their functions are as follows:

> ▶ **New:** New allows you to create a brand new record. In this case, unless you add another experimental group, it is not necessary.

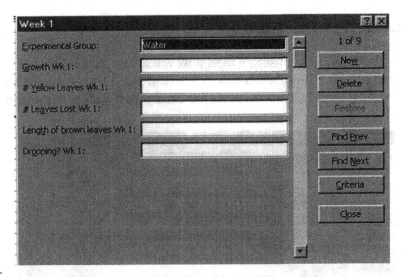

Figure 5.2   Form Mode

▶ **Delete:** Delete allows you to delete an entire record.

▶ **Restore:** You can click Restore before you press **Enter/Return** to undo any changes that you made to the record and return it to its previous values.

▶ **Find Previous:** Find Previous finds the previous record in the list. When used in conjunction with the criteria feature, Find Previous will find the previous record in a list based on the specified criteria.

▶ **Find Next:** Find Next finds the next record in the list. When used in conjunction with the criteria feature, Find Next will find the next record in a list based on the specified criteria.

▶ **Criteria:** This is a very powerful feature that actually has its own menu. This menu and its options will be explained in detail in the next section.

▶ **Close:** The close button will close the form and take you back to the main spreadsheet (or list).

Entering Information

Entering information using a form now becomes a simple process. You simply input the information about each field for each experiment. After you complete each "record," press the **Enter/Return** key to move on.

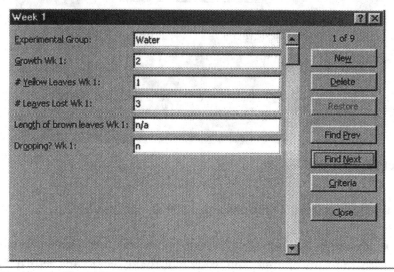

Figure 5.3   Form Mode Week 1

Complete your first week's database with the following information:

Experimental Group	Growth Wk 1	# Yellow Leaves Wk 1	# Leaves Lost Wk 1	Length of brown leaves Wk 1	Drooping? Wk 1
Water	2	1	3	n/a	n
Soil	0	1	2	n/a	n
None	0	5	10	n/a	y
Normal Fertilizer	3	0	0	n/a	n
Excess Fertilizer	0	4	6	n/a	y
No Fertilizer	1	0	1	n/a	n
Light	1	0	2	n/a	n
Moderate Light	0	2	1	n/a	n
No Light	0	3	3	n/a	y

Figure 5.4   Week 1 Database

The Criteria Feature

At first glance, when you click on the Criteria button, it looks identical to the form.

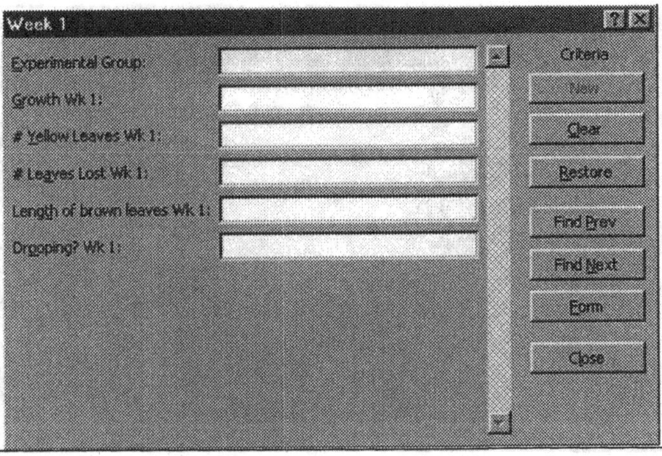

Figure 5.5   The Criteria Feature

However, with the criteria feature, you are not altering the database. Rather, you are specifying criteria to find something specific within the database.

In Figure 5.6, you are looking for plants that aren't doing very well. You are seaching for plants with a growth rate of less than one (inch, centimeter, etc.), that are drooping ("y" for "yes," for example). When you press **Enter/Return**, you are automatically taken to the next record in the list that matches the specified criteria. (See Figure 5.7.)

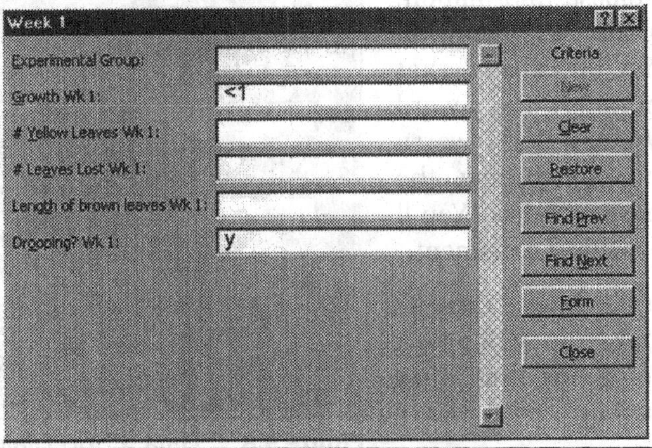

Figure 5.6   Criteria Search for Growth and Drooping

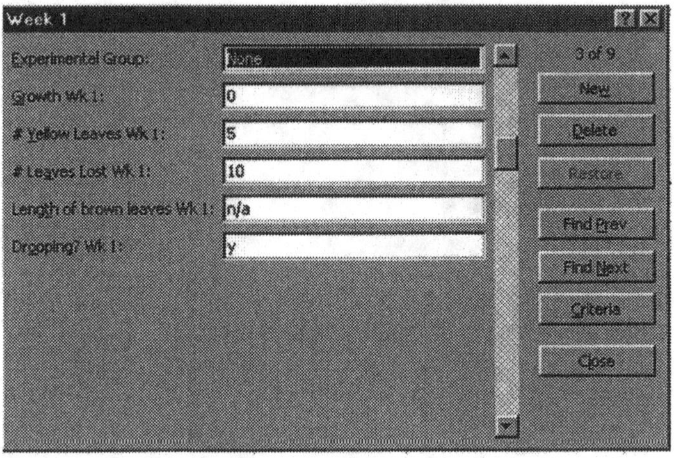

Figure 5.7   Record With Matched Criteria

Sorting

Another option is to not use the form feature but instead sort by certain criteria. Although not as powerful, it is an easy way to "rearrange" the data so that you can order information for a specific purpose. This is often used to reorder information alphabetically or numerically. Let's try sorting with our example:

1. Click in the first cell that contains your database information. In this case, you will click on cell A3 that contains the word "Water." Don't worry about including the column titles. You'll see why in a moment.

2. Next, choose **Data > Sort**. You will see a dialog box that looks like this:

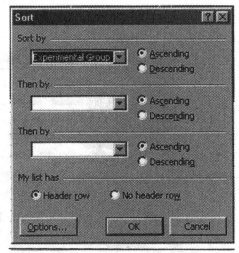

Figure 5.8   Data > Sort Dialog Box

You will notice that Excel automatically indicates your column titles. Look at the area near the bottom of the dialog. Notice how the radio button is selected for the "Header Row" option of "My list has." If you did not have column titles, the column titles would be the basic letter "labels" of A, B, C, D, and so on.

3. Use the graphic in Figure 5.9 to determine the sort criteria.

In this case, you will be sorting first by growth in ascending order (from lowest to highest), then by whether or not it is drooping (descending is checked because "n" for "no" comes before "y" for "yes" alphabetically), then by experimental group.

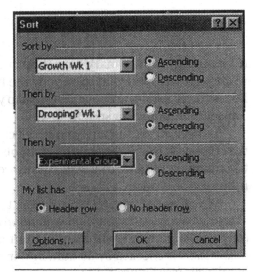

Figure 5.9   Sort Criteria

4. Note: Make sure you *save* before sorting. It is often not easy to "unsort." If you do make a mistake and cannot figure out how to undo what you did, close the file without saving. The file can then be opened from the point of your last save. Click on **OK** to sort your data.

Your data is now sorted. The experimental group in which the plants did not grow are listed first, followed by drooping leaves (yes/no), and finally alphabetically by name of the experimental group itself. In the example, the "excess fertilizer" group had plants that did not grow

	A	B	C	D	E	F
1			Photosynthesis Experiment			
2	Experimental Group	Growth Wk 1	# Yellow Leaves Wk 1	# Leaves Lost Wk 1	Length of brown leaves Wk 1	Drooping? Wk 1
3	Excess Fertilizer	0	4	6	n/a	y
4	No Light	0	8	9	n/a	y
5	None	0	5	10	n/a	y
6	Moderate Light	0	2	1	n/a	n
7	Soil	0	1	2	n/a	n
8	Light	1	0	2	n/a	n
9	No Fertilizer	1	0	1	n/a	n
10	Water	2	1	3	n/a	n
11	Normal Fertilizer	3	0	0	n/a	n

Figure 5.10   Sort Results

and had drooping leaves. The "no light" and "none" (no soil, no water as the growing medium) also experienced the same zero growth/drooping leaves result. Any number of sorting criteria can be used to achieve the desired sort results.

Validating Input

If you really want to make sure that students input the data that you want them to input, you can specify the type of information necessary for each cell. For example, you can set up your database so that they can only input numbers or specific text.

To begin to set this up, simply select the cells or range of cells for which you want to specify criteria. In our case, it is very easy to select the range of B3:B11 that will specify cells that should only contain numbers for growth.

When you set up *validation criteria*, there are three areas to specify. The first is the Settings or data validation criteria. In this case, we want only whole numbers with a minimum of 0 and a maximum of 50. *Ignore blank* is checked by default, but, in our case, we should check for blank cells (see Figure 5.11).

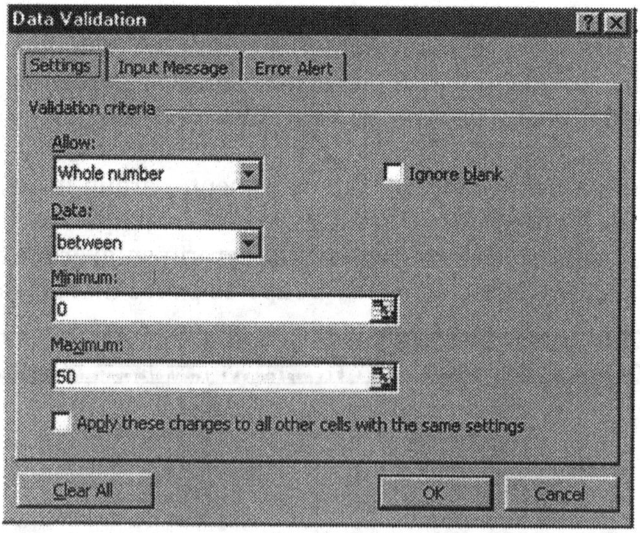

Figure 5.11 Data Validation

The second area is the **Input** criteria. This is a great feature that will allow you to specify a message to be displayed when someone clicks in a cell.

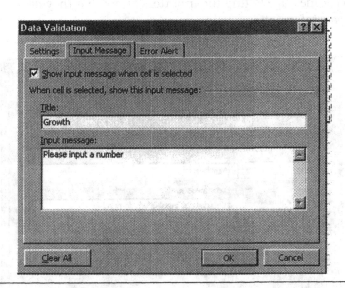

Figure 5.12 Input Message

In our case, the title is reflective of the data that needs to be input. The person inputting is asked to "Please input a number" when that person clicks in the cell.

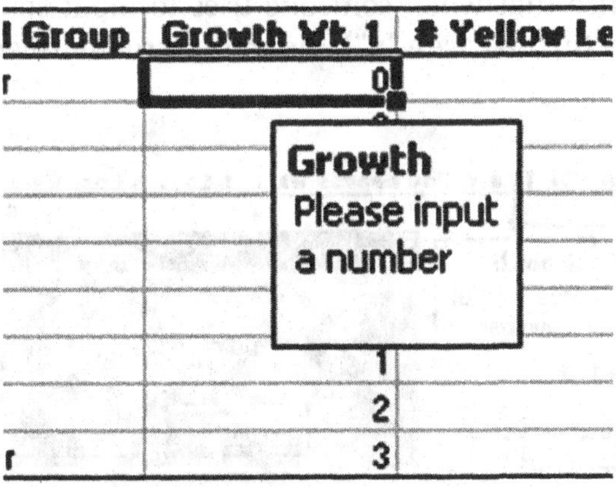

Figure 5.13 Input Message Example

The final area needed is the Error Alert criteria.

In this case, the error alert will be shown when invalid data is entered, the style of graphic is a stop sign, the title is number, and there is an error message letting the inputters know that they did not input the correct information.

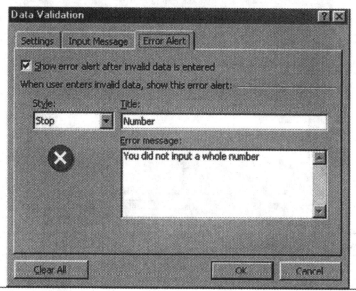

Figure 5.14   Error Alert

You'll notice that when someone tries to input something other than a number (in this case a "y"), the above error message is displayed.

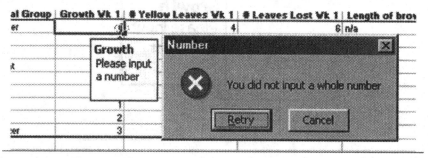

Figure 5.15   Error Alert Example

Quick Review

▶ **Using "Forms" to Input Information:** Choose **Data > Form** and input information one record at a time.

▶ **The Criteria Feature:** Click on the **Criteria** button, input criterion for which to search, press the **Enter/Return** key.

▶ **Sorting:** Save first. Highlight the data to sort. Choose **Data > Sort.** Select columns by which to sort. Select *Sort Order* (ascending, descending). Click on **OK**.

▶ **Validating Data:** Highlight the cell or range of cells. Set the data validation criteria. Select input criteria. Choose the error alert criteria.

6

Creating Charts

Pat is a seventh-grade social science instructor. When the election of 2000 was over, the difficult task of trying to explain what happened was at hand. However, if one just looks at the numbers, they don't seem to tell the whole story.

	A	B	C	D	E
1		Election 2000			
2		Popular Vote Bush/Gore by State			
3		Bush	Gore	Other	Total
4	Alabama	941,173	692,611	32,488	1,666,272
5	Alaska	167,398	79,004	38,090	284,492
6	Arizona	781,652	685,341	65,023	1,532,016
7	Arkansas	472,940	422,768	26,073	921,781
8	California	4,567,429	5,861,203	537,224	10,965,856
9	Colorado	883,748	738,227	119,393	1,741,368
10	Connecticut	561,104	816,659	82,414	1,460,177
11	Delaware	137,288	180,068	10,173	327,529
12	DC	18,073	171,923	11,898	201,894
13	Florida	2,912,790	2,912,253	138,027	5,963,070
14	Georgia	1,419,720	1,116,230	47,258	2,583,208
15	Hawaii	137,845	205,286	24,820	367,951
16	Idaho	336,937	138,637	26,041	501,615
17	Illinois	2,019,421	2,589,026	131,488	4,739,935
18	Indiana	1,245,836	901,980	51,486	2,199,302

Figure 6.1   Election 2000

The purpose of using charts and other visuals in instruction is to simplify information. As one can see from Figure 6.1, the election result numbers are overwhelming. They also do not properly illustrate the interesting phenomenon that occurred.

A chart, such as this pie chart, simplifies complex numerical data. It is easier to visualize just how close the presidential race was when the data is in chart form.

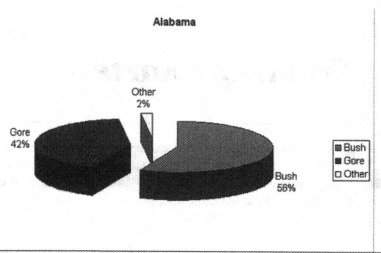

Figure 6.2 Exploding Pie Chart

The Chart Wizard and Chart Types

Microsoft Excel's "Chart Wizard" makes chart creation so simple that students and teachers alike will find it a fairly easy process. Truly, the most difficult part of creating a chart is inputting the data. Even understanding chart types is simplified by the use of the Chart Wizard.

1. **Inputting the data.** This is the most difficult step—only because data entry is time consuming. Data such as the information on the election of 2000 can be found on many governmental Web sites. Then, it is just a matter of typing in the information.

	A	B	C	D	E
1		Election 2000			
2		Popular Vote Bush/Gore by State			
3		Bush	Gore	Other	Total
4	Alabama	941,173	692,611	32,488	1,666,272
5	Alaska	167,398	79,004	38,090	284,492
6	Arizona	781,652	685,341	65,023	1,532,016
7	Arkansas	472,940	422,768	26,073	921,781
8	California	4,567,429	5,861,203	537,224	10,965,856
9	Colorado	883,748	738,227	119,393	1,741,368
10	Connecticut	561,104	816,659	82,414	1,460,177
11	Delaware	137,288	180,068	10,173	327,529
12	DC	18,073	171,923	11,898	201,894
13	Florida	2,912,790	2,912,253	138,027	5,963,070
14	Georgia	1,419,720	1,116,230	47,258	2,583,208
15	Hawaii	137,845	205,286	24,820	367,951
16	Idaho	336,937	138,637	26,041	501,615
17	Illinois	2,019,421	2,589,026	131,488	4,739,935
18	Indiana	1,245,836	901,980	51,486	2,199,302

Figure 6.3 Election 2000 Data

It is still important to add titles to the data. Not only does adding titles make it easier to keep track of information, but these titles can then be used with the Chart Wizard to set up your chart.

2. **Highlight** the information that you want to include in the chart.

	A	B	C	D	E
1		Election 2000			
2		Popular Vote Bush/Gore by State			
3		Bush	Gore	Other	Total
4	Alabama	941,173	692,611	32,488	1,666,272
5	Alaska	167,398	79,004	38,090	284,492
6	Arizona	781,652	685,341	65,023	1,532,016
7	Arkansas	472,940	422,768	26,073	921,781
8	California	4,567,429	5,861,203	537,224	10,965,856
9	Colorado	883,748	738,227	119,393	1,741,368
10	Connecticut	561,104	816,659	82,414	1,460,177
11	Delaware	137,288	180,068	10,173	327,529
12	DC	18,073	171,923	11,898	201,894
13	Florida	2,912,790	2,912,253	138,027	5,963,070
14	Georgia	1,419,720	1,116,230	47,258	2,583,208
15	Hawaii	137,845	205,286	24,820	367,951
16	Idaho	336,937	138,637	26,041	501,615
17	Illinois	2,019,421	2,589,026	131,488	4,739,935
18	Indiana	1,245,836	901,980	51,486	2,199,302

Figure 6.4 Highlight Chart Information

One will notice that the total was not included in this example. Depending on the type of chart that is used, one might want to include the total number of votes.

3. **Use the Chart Wizard.**

   The **Chart Wizard** icon is located on the upper right-hand side of the formatting toolbar. Click on the **Chart Wizard** icon to step through the process of creating a chart.

4. **Chart Wizard, Step 1:**

   When you click on each of the chart types, a description of the chart and how it is to be used appears. In Figures 6.5 and 6.6, a pie chart is used to compare values to a total whereas a line chart is used to display data over time.

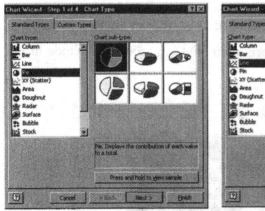 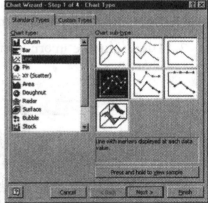

Figures 6.5 and 6.6   Chart Wizard—Chart Type

For the election example, one would not want to use a line chart because the values to compare are not over time. Rather, the values should be compared to a total.

The next step is to select a Chart sub-type.

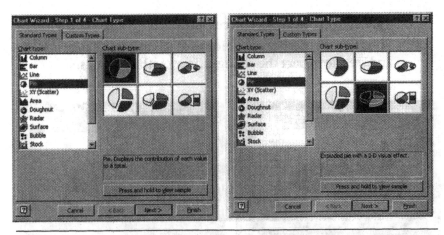

Figures 6.7 and 6.8   Chart Wizard Pie Chart

The basic pie chart compares values to a total but is two dimensional. The exploded pie with 3-D visual effect is popular because the visual impact is greater.

Once the Chart type and Chart sub-type are selected, click on **Next**.

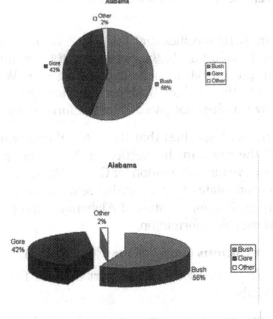

Figure 6.9   Basic Pie Versus 3-D Exploded Pie

5. **Specifying the Chart Source Data** (Step 2 of the Chart Wizard)

   This step can be a bit tricky. However, it is easy to change options and see the impact the changes have on the chart itself.

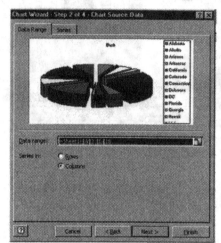 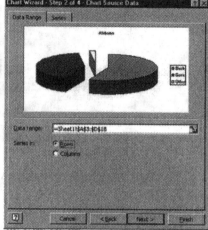

Figures 6.10 and 6.11   Chart Wizard—Source Data

Figure 6.10 specifies that the data information should come from the columns. In the election of 2000 example, using columns gives us visual information for George W. Bush as compared to the total for Bush on just those few states. Unfortunately, this does not give us usable information.

Figure 6.11 specifies that the data information should come from the rows. In the election of 2000 example, using rows gives us visual information for George W. Bush, Al Gore, and all other candidates. One can easily see what piece of the voting pie each received for the state of Alabama. This option give us the most useable information.

6. **Chart Options** (Step 3 of the Chart Wizard)

   There are three sections for Chart Options: Titles, Legend, and Data Labels.

   The title section may or may not be filled out automatically, depending on whether or not the titles in the data source were highlighted initially. If the titles do not show, click on the **Titles** tab to create your titles.

The **Legend** section gives options for the placement of the legend. A legend is a box that identifies patterns or colors assigned to the data series or categories in a chart. You can also choose to not show the legend.

The data labels section gives one many options.

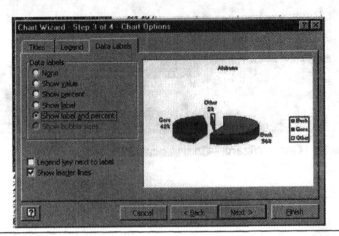

Figure 6.12 Chart Wizard—Legend

The *None* option does not put any labels next to the pie pieces.

Show value shows the exact numeric values for each category.

Show percentage shows the percentage of each piece compared to the total number values.

Show label shows the legend labels next to each pie piece.

Show label and percent shows both the percentage values and the legend labels next to each pie piece (as illustrated).

7. **Chart Location** (Step 4 of the Chart Wizard)

In this final step, one decides where to place the chart.

One can place the chart either as an object in a worksheet (much like inserting a graphic) or as a new sheet within the workbook. The advantage of placing the chart within the sheet is that it can be printed on the same page as the data. The advantage of placing the chart in its own worksheet is that it is a separate sheet that can be printed separately. It's also easier to keep track of the chart when it is in a separate sheet.

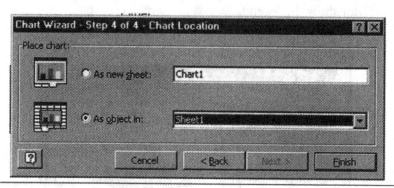

Figure 6.13   Chart Wizard—Chart Location

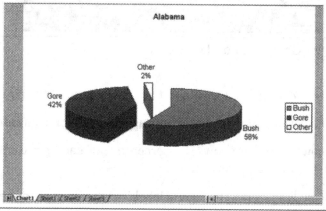

Figure 6.14   3-D Exploded Pie Chart

Troubleshooting Charts

Although the Chart Wizard does provide detailed step-by-step instructions, one can still make a mistake, as there are so many options. One of the most common mistakes is to choose the wrong chart type.

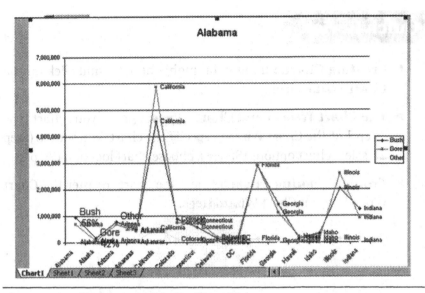

Figure 6.15 Example of Wrong Chart Type

Using the same data from the election of 2000, one can see what happens if a line chart (for time data) is used. The chart is a confusing mess. Not to worry. It is easy to fix.

If Your Chart Is in Its Own Sheet

In Figure 6.15, the chart has been placed into its own sheet. To change the chart type, simply click on the sheet that contains the chart and click on the **Chart Wizard** icon. Then, repeat the same steps to choose another chart type. On the 4th step (Chart Location), make certain that you choose the same chart number to replace the old, erroneous chart. If you choose a higher numbered chart (such as Chart 2), you will have two charts—one erroneous and one correct chart.

If Your Chart Is Embedded Within the Sheet

The steps are essentially the same. The main difference is that instead of clicking on the separate chart sheet, you will click on the chart itself. Then, click on the **Chart Wizard** icon and repeat the same steps to choose another chart type.

Quick Review

▶ **Creating Charts:** Input data, highlight data, and click on the **Chart Wizard** icon.

▶ **The Chart Wizard and Chart Types:** Choose your chart type (Step 1 of the Chart Wizard), specify the chart data source (Step 2), select chart options (Step 3), choose chart location (Step 4).

▶ **Troubleshooting Charts:** Select the chart, reenter the Chart Wizard, repeat Chart Wizard steps.

![Excel icon] **7**

Printing an Excel Worksheet or Workbook

Setting Up the Page

You can determine the appearance of your printed sheets by changing the options in the Page Setup dialog box. You can adjust any of the margins, including the header and footer margins. You can add a customized header(s) or footer(s). You can also center the data vertically and/or horizontally.

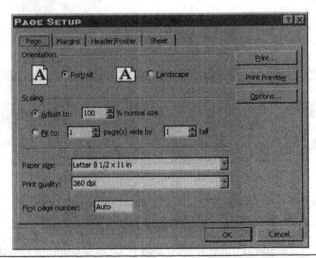

Figure 7.1   Page Setup Dialog Box for Microsoft Excel (PC)

83

1. Click on **File > Page Setup**.

2. To set the margins, click on the **Margins** tab. In the Top, Bottom, Left, Right, and Header and Footer boxes, enter the measurements for the margins you want.

You can also center the data vertically and/or horizontally while you are in the *Margins* dialog box. Under the *Center On Page*, choose the option you want—you can check vertical and/or horizontal.

3. To add or edit headers and/or footers, click on the **Header/Footer** tab. You can select the headers and footers you want in the *Header* and *Footer* boxes, or you can create a custom header and/or footer.

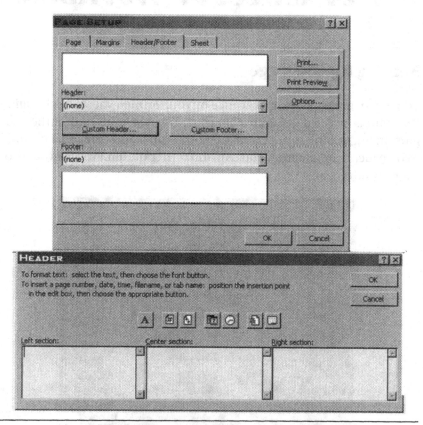

Figure 7.2   Header/Footer Dialog Box (PC) and Custom Header Dialog Box (PC)

4. To set the page orientation, click on the **Page** tab (see Figure 7.1). Now, under *Orientation*, click on either *Portrait* or *Landscape*. Usually, if you are printing out the spreadsheet itself, you will choose a landscape orientation to get more of the columns on the page. If you are setting up a page of data with a graph or chart, you might prefer the portrait orientation.

What to Print

You need to determine what you want to print—all the worksheet, which may have a chart or graphic on it, just part of the worksheet, the entire workbook (more than one worksheet), gridlines or not, row and column headings or not. You can also specify rows or columns that will appear as titles on every page (if the worksheet takes more than one page to print all the data). All this can be specified in the *Page Setup* dialog box.

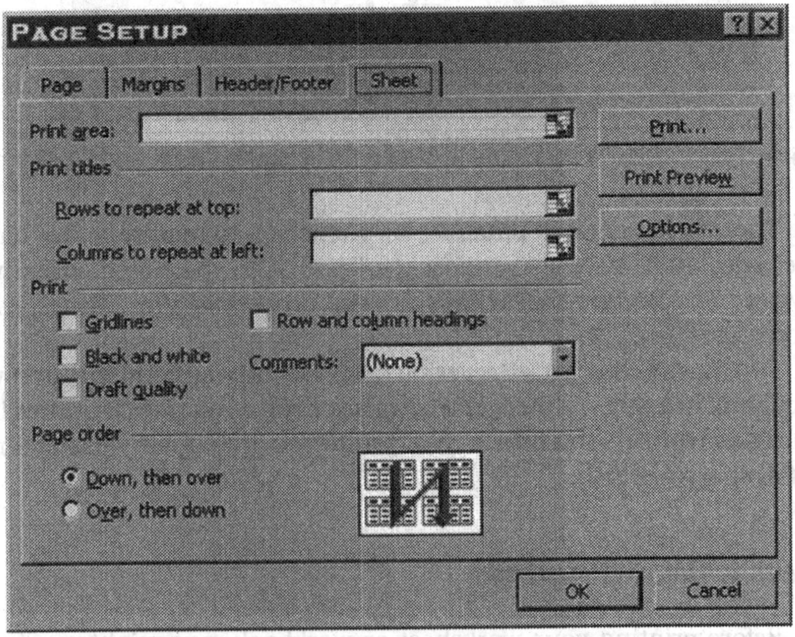

Figure 7.3 Specifying What to Print

To specify a range in the worksheet that you want printed, select **File > Page Setup** and click on the **Sheet** tab. Enter the range you want to print. You can't just put down "b" for the column to print, or "3" for the row to print—you must specify the portion of the column or row. You do that by typing the beginning cell, a colon, and then the last cell (see Figure 7.4).

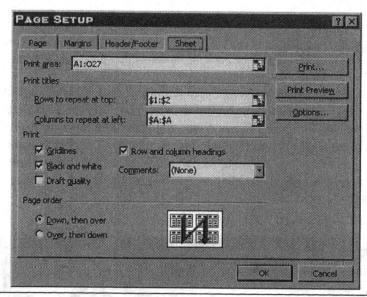

Figure 7.4. Specifying Printing Area and Titles for Rows and Columns

There is not enough data on this worksheet to require more than one page, but if there were, under the *Print Titles*, you would enter the row and/or column ranges that you want printed as titles. This is also shown in Figure 7.4.

Finally, you can check the various boxes if you want gridlines or row or column headings printed. You can also check if you want it printed in black and white (if you have a color printer) or draft quality (faster and not as sharp a print).

Preview Before Printing

Before printing your worksheet or workbook, you might want to preview what it will look like. You can click on **Print Preview** or select

File > Print Preview. Figure 7.5 shows what part of one of the spreadsheets from Chapter 3 looks like using Print Preview.

In Print Preview, click on **Margins** if you want to adjust the margins, using the drag handles (the small black boxes). The cursor becomes a magnifying glass. If you click, it will magnify a portion of the page or return the display to the whole page.

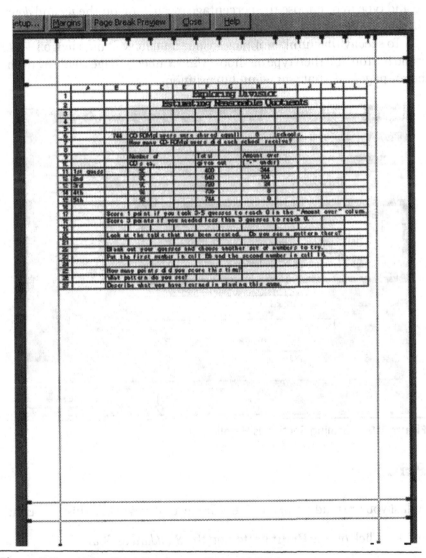

Figure 7.5   Using Print Preview to Change Margins

Making the Spreadsheet Fit the Page

If the spreadsheet is larger or smaller than you want it to be when it prints, you have a couple of options—you can scale your work to fit more or fewer pages than it would at normal size, or you can specify the number of pages for the finished print job. To enlarge or reduce your printed data, select the **File > Page Setup > Page**. Then click on *Adjust to* and type in or choose the percentage by clicking on the *up* and *down* arrows to the right of the box.

To specify the number of pages your data must fit on, click on *Fit to* radio button and then type or choose the number of pages wide by number of pages tall that you want it to print on.

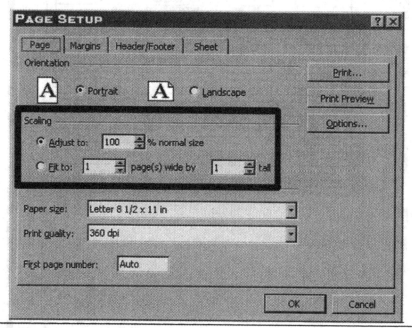

Figure 7.6   Scaling Section Is Highlighted

Printing

At last you are ready to print. There are several ways to do this. You can:

1. Click on the **Print** button on the *Standard* toolbar.

2. Click on **Print** in the **File** menu.

3. Click on the **Print** button in the **Print Preview** window.

4. Click on the **Print** button in the *Page Setup* dialog box.

If you choose option 1, printing begins immediately. Microsoft Excel will use whatever the current settings in the *Page Setup* and *Print* dialog boxes happen to be. If you want to print only a selected portion of the spreadsheet or you want to change the margins or the page orientation, you will need to use option 2.

If your spreadsheet consists of several sheets, you learned in Chapter 1 that it is called a workbook. If you want to print the entire workbook, you need to click on the *Entire Workbook* in the *Print* dialog box.

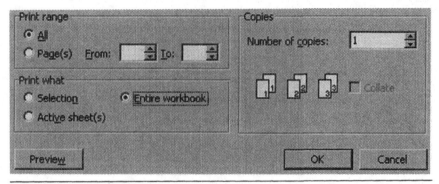

Figure 7.7   Print Dialog Box—Printing Multiple Worksheets (Entire Workbook)

Quick Review

▶ **Selecting a Printer:**

    WIN: Select **File > Print.** Click the **Printer** button and select the printer.

    MAC: Select **Apple menu > Chooser.** Select the printer, then **File > Print.**

▶ **Setting Up the Page: File > Page Setup.** Set margins, headers, footers, page orientation from the separate tabs in the *Page Setup* dialog box.

▶ **What to Print: File > Page Setup** and select the **Sheet** tab, Enter the range you want to print by typing the beginning cell, a colon, and then the last cell (see Figure 7.6). Check your selection and make final adjustments in Print Preview.

▶ **Making the Spreadsheet Fit the Page: File > Page Setup** and select the **Page** tab, choose the *Adjust to* or *Fit to* radio buttons, make your selection(s), and click **OK**.

▶ **Printing:** Clicking on the **Print** button on the *Standard* toolbar, or select **File > Print**. Print icons are also located in the **Print Preview** window and the *Page Setup* dialog boxes.

Index